THE MANISCHEWITZ PASSOVER COOKBOOK

WALKER AND COMPANY
NEW YORK

The Manischewitz Passover Cookbook

BY
DEBORAH ROSS

ILLUSTRATED BY GENE SZAFRAN

A James B. Adler, Inc. book

*Text, new recipes, compilation, and index
Copyright © 1969 by The B. Manischewitz Company.
Illustrations Copyright © 1969 by Walker and Company.*

*Other recipes Copyright © 1957, 1958,
1959, 1960, 1961, 1962, 1963, 1964, 1965,
1966, 1967, 1968 by The B. Manischewitz Company.*

*All rights reserved. No part of this book may be
reproduced or transmitted in any form or by
any means, electronic or mechanical, including
photocopying, recording, or by any information storage
and retrieval system without permission
in writing from the Publisher.*

*First published in the United States of America
in 1969 by Walker and Company,
a division of the Walker Publishing Company, Inc.*

*Published simultaneously in Canada
by The Ryerson Press, Toronto.*

Library of Congress Catalog Card Number: 69-14565

Printed in the United States of America

Designed by Arthur Hawkins

CONTENTS	PAGE
INTRODUCTION	4
PASSOVER	16
APPETIZERS AND SOUPS	38
MEATS	52
POULTRY	76
"OTHER MEALS" MAIN DISHES	90
FRIED THINGS	106
SALADS, DRESSINGS, AND RELISHES	118
VEGETABLES AND SIDE DISHES	128
BAKED THINGS	146
SWEET THINGS	174
RECIPE INDEX	183

THE
MANISCHEWITZ
PASSOVER
COOKBOOK

INTRODUCTION

JEWISH COOKERY AS IT REFLECTS JEWISH LIFE

Do you have a lopsided view of Jewish cookery? Then you are not alone. Most people assume that what Mama cooks is what all Jewish mamas cook. Not so! The cookery in the Jewish community is the cookery of the world, because Jews have lived in every country of the world and in each have learned to cook in the style of that country. Thus, Polish Jewish cooking is quite different from Romanian Jewish. Even more dissimilar is the cooking of a North African Jew.

To understand these differences, it is necessary to trace Jewish history back to the year 70 C.E., when the Romans destroyed the Second Temple and dispersed the Jews to wander and settle all over the world. The majority went to either Germany or Spain. Today's Ashkenazim can trace their ancestry to the German group; Sephardim trace theirs to the Spanish.

As a result, the roots of Ashkenazi cooking are German. Knaidlach, gefilte fish, kugelen, mandelbrodt, and other such dishes that most Ashkenazim make are based on German specialties.

You might expect, therefore, that Sephardic cooking would be based on Spanish cuisine, but you would be wrong. Large numbers of Sephardim settled in the Middle East and North Africa after the Spanish Inquisition and expulsion forced them to flee Spain in the late fifteenth century. Because Turkey dominated that part of the world, the cooking of these people is basically Turkish in origin. Borscht, blintzes, kreplach, matzo balls, kugelen, sweet-and-sour stuffed cabbage, lox bagel, and all the other foods that Ashkenazim consider typically Jewish, these people have never made. Sephardic cooking is marked by such delights as dolma (stuffed grape leaves), moussaka (an eggplant main dish), falafel (chick-pea-patty sandwich), homos and tahina (chick-peas and sesame-seed paste dressing), feta cheese (goat cheese), yogurt, pita (Middle Eastern bread), baklava (a rich pastry made of nuts, honey, and phyllo pastry), and endless other Turkish-inspired dishes. However, the Sephardim of Italy, Holland, Spain, and other European countries cook in the styles of these lands, while Turkish influence is evident in the cuisine of Ashkenazim of several European countries.

Eggplant relish, so dear to people in the once-Turkish lands of the Middle East and North Africa, is also a Romanian meichel (treat). The strudel of Hungary started out as baklava, and even the dough is similar to the phyllo pastry used for this Turkish meichel. Because the Hungarians had plentiful fruits, they gradually decreased the customary sweetened nut filling and substituted fruits. However, nut strudel can be traced directly to the rolled form of baklava; only the syrup is omitted. The layered version became in Ashkenazi cooking fluden (or fladen or floden if you wish).

Yet Jewish cookery differs from purely Turkish, or African, or European cuisine because in every country Jews have adapted dishes to fit their taste and observance of Kashruth. They use the local foods because they are the most plentiful, the easiest to obtain, and the best suited to the climate and way of life. But creative Jewish women changed the original recipes to make them suitable for the kosher home. For instance, a popular Hungarian delicacy is Chicken Paprikash. Jewish women, first hearing of this dish, were interested until they learned that in the last step sour cream is added. For most, this meant that the recipe had to be ignored. But the creative homemaker met the challenge. She followed the original recipe and simply omitted the sour cream. The result was the Hungarian Jewish meichel, Chicken Paprika. Multiply this procedure by thousands of recipes and numerous adventurous cooks in all the countries of the world, and you have the story of what is now known as Jewish cookery.

While there are few recipes that cannot be traced to some previous source, certain dishes have become associated with particular groups of people. Foods created by Jews for Jews were always originated to fill a religious requirement or to symbolize a holiday celebration. Particularly valuable were the dishes created to be served hot on the Sabbath without breaking the rule against cooking during the day of rest. The classic dish in this group is known in the United States as cholent. This forerunner of the modern casserole serves the Sabbath needs so well that some form of the dish has appeared in every country where Jews have lived. The names and recipes for this concoction are as diverse as the countries of Asia, Africa, and Europe. Basically the dish is made with some kind of meat or poultry, some variety of beans, and one or more starchy foods. Often vegetables are added. While recipes are as individual as people, the European versions usually contain beef, beans, barley, and potatoes. In Asia and Africa, where beef, barley, and potatoes are not staples, the dish is made with lamb or chicken, rice, and beans.

No matter the country, women prepare this casserole dish on Friday before sundown. Tightly covered, the pan is placed in a warm oven, where it remains until needed on Saturday after morning synagogue services. Years ago, the cholent was taken to the town baker. His ovens were banked for the Sabbath, and the low temperature was just what the women needed. Each had to make a special mark on her pot to be sure no one got the wrong meal by mistake.

Especially interesting are the symbolic values assigned to foods now traditional for holidays and festivals. The food customs for Rosh Hashanah are particularly intricate. Fish, preferably in the form of gefilte fish, is always served, because it is the symbol of fruitfulness and plenty. By custom, the head of the fish is served to the head of the house as a symbol of his leadership and wisdom, but it also symbolizes the head, or beginning, of the New Year.

The Prophet Nehemiah commanded for Rosh Hashanah, "Eat of the fat and drink of the sweet." For this reason, rich and sweet foods are the order of the day. They symbolize the wish for prosperity and a sweet New Year. Sliced apples and pieces of challah are dipped in honey and eaten at the beginning of a meal. Honey cake is served by almost all Jews, as is some form of tzimmes. For Rosh Hashanah, the carrots for tzimmes should be cut into rounds to resemble coins, symbolizing the wish for prosperity, and sweetened with honey for a sweet New Year. Bitter or sour foods are avoided to ward off such influences.

Fruits and vegetables also have important significance at Rosh Hashanah. On the second night of the holiday, a new fruit, not previously eaten that year, is served, and a special prayer, a "Shehecheyanu," is recited over it. Frequently a pomegranate is used for this purpose, because its many seeds symbolize fruitfulness. Sephardic Jews eat beets at least once during the holiday, because they are one of the ten foods blessed at the Rosh Hashanah table. No discussion of Rosh Hashanah food customs could end without mention of the round challahs used at the table. They symbolize a wish for a complete year in which there will be no break or interruption. The tops of these challahs are frequently decorated with ladders or birds made of dough. These will provide a means for the wishes and prayers to reach the heavens.

On erev Yom Kippur, it is a mitzvah (religious duty) to serve lavish meals. It is also a custom on this day before Yom Kippur to serve fish and kreplach soup at the noontime meal. The pre-fast meal, served in time to be finished before sunset on the day before Yom Kippur, must be carefully planned or there will be undue suffering the following day. All food should be underseasoned, and salty foods must be avoided, because they increase thirst. At the beginning of the meal, as on Rosh Hashanah, each person eats a piece of challah or apple dipped in honey. Fish is avoided because it increases thirst. Noodle soup is traditional, as is poultry and simply prepared vegetables, salads, and desserts. After the meal, the entire family attends Kol Nidre services at the synagogue or temple.

On Yom Kippur, at the end of the Holy Day services, after wishing each other a gmar chatima tova (a favorable verdict), the congregants go home to break the fast. This meal varies widely, depending on national origin and family custom. Many people serve a dairy smorgasbord-type meal, with herring, smoked fish, eggs, cheeses, and blintzes. The herring, marinate, and other salty, spicy foods are especially refreshing after the long fast. The salt helps the body, dehydrated by the abstinence from fluids as well as foods, to return to normal quickly. Greek Jews frequently have the famous Greek Lemon Chicken Soup to begin the festive Yom Kippur night dinner. Sephardic Jews in Turkey, Greece, Iraq, and other countries often break the fast with almond milk (called mizo, soubya, or soumade), which is made by pounding blanched almonds until smooth and adding water. Light and nourishing, it is symbolic, because of its whiteness, of the purity that follows after Yom Kippur prayers. The Jews of Syria traditionally break the fast with a light meal of soft-cooked eggs (as a symbol that the current year has just begun) and kayek (salt sesame) biscuits, instead of bread.

During Succoth, the Feast of Booths as well as the Festival of the Harvest, the word "rejoicing" is the key to the celebration, and sumptuous meals are an important part of the picture. As on Rosh Hashanah and erev Yom Kippur, at the beginning of the meals, a blessing is said on a piece of challah dipped in honey. There are no special regulations concerning the dishes to be cooked, but it is customary to serve fruits and vegetables as symbols of the harvest. On Simchas Torah, the last day of this festival, tradition specifies a lavish meal, featuring turkey.

Latkes are traditional fare for Chanukah because it is believed that the wives of the Maccabees fed latkes, or pancakes, to the fighters, as a meal that could be prepared quickly. Others also believe that the oil in which latkes are fried is symbolic of the single cruse of oil that burned for eight days. The type of latke varies with the national origin of the family. Potato is popular with Jews from Central and Eastern Europe. In Israel, rice pancakes or fritters, cornmeal cakes, and corn fritters are commonly prepared. However, buckwheat cakes are especially favored by French, Polish, and Russian immigrants in Israel. The Swiss, on the other hand, prefer delicate apple fritters.

Cheese dishes on Chanukah owe their traditional popularity to Judith of Bethulia. It is reported that this brave woman entertained Holfernes, a leader of enemy troops that held her city in siege, and fed him quantities of cheese to make him thirsty. To quench this thirst, he drank much wine, grew sleepy, and was easily defeated. Some people combine the traditional latkes with cheese and serve these cheese pancakes with sour cream in celebration of the holiday.

Purim, one of the gayest holiday celebrations, is also connected with picturesque culinary customs. The story of Esther is of course the basis for many of the Purim customs. Because she fasted for three days before she pleaded with King Ahasuerus, the day before Purim is observed as the Fast of Esther. Jews eat chick-peas (nahit) and fava beans (bub) during Purim to emulate Queen Esther, who ate legumes instead of meat because she observed the rules of Kashruth and King Ahasuerus' kitchens were not kosher. Esther's Hebrew name was Hadassah, and the worldwide women's organization, which was established on Purim, was named after her.

Throughout the world, pastries and cookies, symbolic of Haman, are baked for Purim. Most people in the United States have hamantaschen, the tricornered pastries filled with poppy seeds or prunes, to look like Haman's hat. Kreplach are also served because they are triangular. In Holland, cookies are cut in the shape of a man—Haman—and baked for the children. The Viennese bake "Kindel," which look like babies tied in blankets, as a symbol of Haman's large family.

One of the most charming customs of the holiday derives from Mordecai's order to make Purim a time to send "portions to one another" (Shalach monas). These gifts are always foods that are ready to serve—candies, confections, fruits, and wines. Each woman, of course, takes this opportunity to display her culinary and artistic ability.*

There are several possible explanations for the wide use of dairy foods on Shavuoth. Some say that it is because the Jews waited so long for Moses to come down from Mount Sinai that they were very hungry and prepared a dairy meal to avoid waiting for meat to be cooked. A second version says that the Law is compared to milk and honey, so dairy dishes are served. Yet another theory is that until they received

---

*Passover, which is the next holiday, is discussed on pages 16-35.

the Law, the Jews did not eat kosher meats. There was no time to slaughter and kosher meats immediately after receiving the Law, so they ate dairy.

Whatever the reason, dairy dishes are the suitable ones to prepare at this time. Especially popular are noodle or matzo and cheese kugels, cheese latkes, blintzes, cheese cakes, cheese knishes, cheese strudel, cheese kreplach, and pirogen. Jews from Alsace-Lorraine make a cheese-onion tart (Quiche Lorraine), which is a true delicacy. Jews from the Middle East and other countries where Sephardic Jews live always serve white rice, to symbolize purity, with the dairy products.

Sephardic Jews from Italy, Greece, and Turkey bake Mount Sinai cookies, shaped like cones to resemble mountains. Each cookie is topped with a walnut half to symbolize the dark cloud that hung over Mount Sinai when the Law was being given to Moses. The Viennese also bake Mount Sinai symbols, but they make them of puff pastry, with a cheese filling, and shape them to look like mountains. The dark cloud is a topping of plum jam. The joy of the people at receiving the Law is simply expressed in the foods they eat in commemoration.

Other important foods for Shavuoth are the first yields of the harvest —both fruits and vegetables—which are served in a wide variety of salads, desserts, and side dishes.

In addition to the international nature of Jewish cookery, the influence of Kashruth regulations, and the development of special dishes to fit religious and holiday needs, there is one other significant factor to be considered—economy. In the late nineteenth and early twentieth centuries, large numbers of Jews, mainly from Eastern Europe, fled their homelands because of oppression, bigotry, and poverty. Arriving in the United States, the average family moved into two or three unheated rooms, probably without running water. Papa went to work for the lowest salary of that time, and, in addition, the family probably had someone still in Europe in need of help and who must eventually be brought to the United States.

When people are at the bottom of the economic scale, yet their tradition dictates that they must provide education for the children and tzedakah (justice or righteousness) for the needy, they become experts in making every penny count. These women wasted no food, made four to five tempting offerings from one chicken, used low-cost staples most of the time, and stretched expensive ingredients with inexpensive ones to make them go farther. Just think about your favorite Jewish dishes. Isn't almost every one of them filled, stuffed, rolled in a dough, encased in a potato mixture, or extended in some other way?

How did Jews change from being the most careful of spenders with the food budget to their current near-traditional lavishness? Blame the Mama and the Bubeh (grandmother)—but not too much. They meant well. If you can imagine not having enough food to keep your children from going to bed hungry, then you can understand what happened as the financial situation eased. Papa aided and abetted Mama. When he was a child, only a rich man's family could be fat. Who else could afford that much food? "Ess, ess." Papa provided the money and Mama went on buying sprees at the butcher shop, live poultry market, appetizing store, bakery, grocery, and vegetable stands. Mountains of fragrant, wondrous delights poured into the house and thence to the table. Mama no sooner cleared the table after breakfast than she was planning "what should be for lunch," and then for supper. In between, of course, came tea and cake, a "light snack" to tide everyone over, and before bedtime, at least a little piece of something with a glass of milk. How could you sleep if you were hungry?

From all this fürachtz (dealings) came problems for following generations—fighting the battle of the bulge. Young mothers today rarely want their children to be chubby. It is with the grandmothers that the problem still persists. They do not raise too much fuss with their own daughters, because, after all, they are brilliant and would not harm the children. But their sons' wives—that's another story. "She's starving my grandchildren. She's too lazy to make a decent meal for them. Look how skinny they are."

HOW TO USE THE BOOK

Now that you have been convinced that you can use recipes not only from landtsleit (people from the same country of origin) but also from the combined cuisine of the world, it is time to talk about the recipes in this book. If you were to be offered only the traditional Passover recipes that your mothers and grandmothers made, this would be a pamphlet. If you were offered all the recipes that could be made for Passover, this would be an encyclopedia. Neither alternative seemed suitable. For this book only gems have been selected, each thoroughly tested and tasted, to enhance your eisheth chail crown (homemaker's laurels).

For your own sake, trust the directions given throughout this book. Every recipe has been thoroughly tested and turns out a perfect dish if you follow the instructions.

GETTING STARTED

1. Always read the entire recipe through before starting. You do not want any surprises once you start to cook.

2. Be sure you have all the ingredients and in the amounts required.

3. Get out all the equipment needed.

4. If a baking pan is to be used, prepare it as instructed in the recipe.

5. Measure all ingredients called for and line them up in the order in which they will be used.

6. If the oven is to be used, preheat it.

7. Do not change a recipe even to cut or double it unless you are a very experienced cook.

MEASURING

1. Always use standard measuring equipment. A set of measuring cups and spoons costs very little, yet the lack of them is one of the major causes of cooking failures.

2. Always use level measurements. To measure dry ingredients, fill the measuring cup or spoon to overflowing and then level it off with the straight edge of a table knife or spatula.

3. To measure liquids, use a standard glass measuring cup marked off in quarters and thirds.

4. To measure butter or margarine, remember that a ¼-pound stick is equal to ½ cup.

5. Do not use whipped butter or margarine in any of these recipes. They contain air, so a cup of these whipped products contains less fat than the unwhipped ones.

6. To measure honey, proceed as for liquids. Be sure to get all the honey out of the measuring cup with a rubber scraper.

SELECTING POTS AND PANS

1. Always use the type and size of pot or pan specified. Failure to do so may result in disaster.

2. If a recipe calls for a tightly covered pot, it is important to use one. Otherwise, there is undesired evaporation.

3. If you are about to purchase new pots and pans, buy the very best you can afford. They are worth the money if you are paying for quality rather than gimmicks.

4. Always use a tube pan with a removable center tube. Otherwise it is almost impossible to get a cake out of the pan intact.

OVEN TEMPERATURES

Always use the exact temperature specified in a recipe. Years ago, women tested oven temperature by putting a little mound of flour inside. If it browned in one minute, the oven was hot, two minutes meant a moderate oven, and three indicated a slow oven. Of course you had to see this demonstrated by an experienced cook, because, "What means brown?" There have been other hit-or-miss methods through the years, and one home economist swears by a method she accidentally discovered, maintaining she can tell immediately if an oven is hotter than 350°F. When she looks into the oven and melting mascara causes her eyelashes to stick together, she knows the oven is too hot. Caution: she has used one brand of mascara for many years and professes not to know if her test will work with other makes.

Because most ovens have thermostatic controls, even the novice in the kitchen can relax about baking and roasting these days. However, there is one catch. Sometimes these controls need readjustment. To avoid problems, it is wise to use a good quality oven thermometer to check each time before using the oven. Also, periodically, ask your local utility company to calibrate the oven. There is usually no charge for this service.

INGREDIENTS

Some of the old adages have survived because they are constant truths. Therefore, you get out of something what you put into it. Poor-quality meat is not improved by cooking. Wilted celery will not suddenly come alive in texture and flavor to give the crunch and taste to a salad. Enough said. It is only fair to tell you that because all of these recipes were developed in the Manischewitz test kitchen, they were made with Manischewitz products. This does not mean that they will not work with other brands, but use them at your own discretion. Particularly where recipes for cake-mix variations are concerned, caution is recommended.

Listed below are those products called for in recipes in this book that are made by Manischewitz.

MATZOS, MATZO PRODUCTS
Matzo
Thin Tea Matzos
Egg Matzos
100% Whole Wheat
Matzo Farfel
Matzo Meal
Matzo Cake Meal
Matzo Cereal

CAKE MIXES
Sponge Cake Mix
Chocolate Cake Mix
　(with Fudge Frosting)
Coffee Cake Mix
Yellow Cake Mix
　(with Fudge Frosting)
Marble Cake Mix
Honey Cake Mix
Pound Cake Mix
Chocolate Brownie Mix
Coconut Macaroon Mix
Chocolate Macaroon Mix
Chocolate Chiffon Cake Mix

CAKES, COOKIES
Fruit Cuts
Mandel Cuts
Marble Mandel Cuts
Chocolate Chip Mandel Loaf

INTRODUCTION

Fruit Filled Mandel Loaf
Marble Mandel Loaf
Cinnamon Raisin Mandel Loaf
Macaroons, Almond Flavor
Macaroons, Chocolate Flavor
Macaroons, Coconut
Macaroons, Honey
Chocolate Covered Coconut Macaroons
Fancy Cookies
Chocolate Chip Cookies
Chocolate Nut Cookies
Almond Cookies
Jelly Top Cookies
Kichel
Jumbo Kichel

SOUPS, BORSCHT
Chicken Soup, Clear
Chicken Soup, Matzo Balls
Beef-Cabbage Soup
Borscht
Borscht, Low Calorie
Schav

GEFILTE FISH
Gefilte Fish
Fishballs
Fishlets
Whitefish-Pike
Deluxe Fishlets
Gefilte Fish, Home-Style (in cans)
Whitefish-Pike, Home-Style (in cans)

PRESERVES
Strawberry
Cherry
Raspberry
Peach
Grape
Orange Marmalade
Seedless Black Raspberry
Pineapple

CANNED FRUITS, JUICES
Sliced Yellow Cling Peaches
Yellow Cling Peaches, Halves
Elberta Peaches, Halves
Fruit Cocktail
Bartlett Pears
Apple Sauce
Cranberry Sauce
Stewed Prunes
Fruit Compote
Apple Juice
Prune Juice
Tomato Juice

GROCERIES, CONDIMENTS
Griddle Cake Mix
Potato Pancake Mix
Potato Starch
Mandlen for Soup
Matzo Balls, Canned
Kosher Pickles
Deluxe Delight
Catsup
Tomato and Mushroom Sauce
Honey
Coffee, All-Purpose
Coffee, Instant
Tea Bags
Candy: Jellied Fruit Slices
Candy: Marmal Jells
Candy: Assorted Hard Candies (in bags)
Cleanser

BABY FOODS
Heart (Strained or Chopped)
Veal (Strained or Chopped)
Liver (Strained or Chopped)
Beef (Strained or Chopped)
Chicken (Strained or Chopped)

MANISCHEWITZ WINES
Traditional Grape Wines
Concord*
Medium Dry Concord
Dry Concord
Extra Heavy Malaga*
Sauterne
Burgundy
Rosé

Traditional Fruit Wines
Blackberry*
Loganberry*
Cherry*
Elderberry*

Premium Grape Wines
Cream Concord*
White Concord
Extra Dry Concord
Royal Rosé

Premium Fruit Wines
Cherry Dalmaja*
Blackberry Hollandia*

Sparkling Wines
Champagne
Pink Champagne
Sparkling Burgundy
Sparkling Concord

*Specially sweetened

INTRODUCTION

The number of foods and cleaning supplies labeled "Kosher for Passover" and packed under strict Rabbinical supervision grows each year. The list now includes:

Aluminum foil, plastic wraps, and plastic bags
Baby meats
Beverages, carbonated
Borscht and schav
Butter
Cake and macaroon mixes
Cakes, cookies, and macaroons
Candies, fancy chocolates, bittersweet
Catsup
Cheese*
Chocolate bars
Chocolate-pudding mix
Coffee
Cranberry sauce
Cream, both sweet and sour
Cleansers of various types
Packaged dates
Detergents
Canned fish
  Kippered herring
  Salmon
  Sardines
  Sprats
  Tomato herring
  Tuna
Frozen fish fillets
Gefilte fish
Pickled herring, herring in wine sauce
Canned and bottled fruits and fruit juices**
Dried fruits
Glazed fruits
Griddle cake mix
Honey
Horseradish
Ice cream, sherbet, ices (mainly in metropolitan areas)
Jams, jellies, and preserves
Lekvar, prune or apricot
Mandlen (soup nuts)
Pareve margarine, regular, unsalted, and unsalted soft
Matzo balls (in cans and jars)
Matzo and matzo products***
Milk
Noodles and egg barley
Nuts
Pickles and relishes
Potato chips
Potato-pancake mix
Potato starch
Frozen poultry
Tomato-and-mushroom sauce
Vegetable shortening and oil
Canned soups
Seasonings and spices
Stuffed cabbage
Sugar
Artificial sweeteners
Fruit syrups
Soap pads, scouring powder, silver polish, kosher soap
Tea
Canned vegetables (a few)
Vinegar, cider
Wines

Deborah Ross

*Cottage cheese, farmer cheese, and cream cheese are generally available with Rabbinical supervision. Outside the major cities, other kosher cheeses for Passover may be difficult to get.

**Of course you know that all fresh fruits and all fresh vegetables, except beans and peas, may be used.

***No flour of any kind may be used in the home. Matzo meal or matzo cake meal, made from baked Passover matzos, are substituted.

PASSOVER

THROUGH THE YEARS AND AROUND THE WORLD

At sundown on the fourteenth day, in the month of Nisan, in the Promised Land, Canaan, over three thousand years ago, the children of Israel encamped in Gilgal on the plains of Jericho to celebrate the Passover. Thus, after wandering forty years in the desert, did the Jews for the first time since the original Passover night in Egypt follow the ordinance, "And they shall eat the flesh in that night, roast with fire, and unleavened bread; with bitter herbs they shall eat it" (Exodus 12:8). The main elements of the celebration have not changed through the ages—the Passover lamb, the unleavened bread, and the bitter herbs. However, the customs surrounding the festivities have varied over the years and around the world.

In Biblical times such celebrations were held at the Temple, and the people from all over the land gathered at the house of the Lord in Jerusalem to keep the Passover. When for a time the Jewish people desecrated the Temple by idolatry, they also turned away from the celebration of Passover and other festivals. However, when Hezekiah became king of Judah, he ordered the purification of the Temple and the priests. At the same time he sent forth a call to the people of Israel to come to the Temple for the holiday. There followed a most memorable Passover. A great congregation gathered in Jerusalem and helped to cleanse the Temple. "And the children of Israel that were present at Jerusalem kept the feast of unleavened bread seven days with great gladness; and the Levites and the priests praised the Lord day by day, singing with loud instruments unto the Lord" (II Chronicles 30:21). So enthralled were the people that the entire congregation decided to celebrate for seven additional days. In the more than two hundred years since the time of Solomon, there had not been such a celebration in Jerusalem.

Even when the Temple was destroyed by the Babylonians, the exiled Jews continued to celebrate Passover. It was to this period that Jews owe some of the most ancient portions of the Haggadah (the story of the miraculous deliverance of Israel from Egyptian slavery). Among them is the Hoh Lochmoh Anyo, recited near the beginning of the Seder. It is then that the head of the house extends the invitation, "Let all those who are hungry enter and eat thereof; and all who are in distress come and celebrate the Passover."

The first reference found to the celebration of part of the Passover service in the home, rather than in a large congregation, was after the building of the Second Temple. Following impressive and solemn rituals at the Temple, the people carried home portions of the Passover lambs. This meat was roasted on outdoor stoves so that all could see their celebration. After eating the meal, they sang psalms into the night. As a sign of their respect and trust, because so many pilgrims were in the city, householders in Jerusalem left their doors unlocked that night. This action was also used as a symbol of their confidence in divine protection, as promised on the very first Passover night in Egypt.

With the destruction of the Second Temple in 70 C.E., and the beginning of the Diaspora, the Passover festival was no longer a nationwide celebration to be held in one central place, but rather essentially a ceremony in the individual home or small community gatherings. It remained the custom at this Seder (order of service) to recite the Haggadah, following the Biblical commandment: "On that day thou shalt tell the story to thy son, saying, 'This is because of that which the Lord did for me that I came forth out of Egypt'" (Exodus 13:8).

The seven-day festival then became an eight-day festival for all Jews living outside Eretz Israel (land of Israel). Before Hillel II drew up and published in 360 C.E. the first Jewish calendar, the people were dependent on the Sanhedrin (High Court) in Jerusalem for announcing the time to celebrate any festival. Fires were lit on hilltops to spread the word. However, because many Jews lived in other lands, messengers had to be sent out to announce the arrival of a holiday or Rosh Chodesh (new moon). Because the Romans frequently interfered with the messengers, and the exact date for the celebration was not always known, people outside Palestine were told to add a day to each holiday to make sure they did not miss the proper day. To this time, Jews living outside of Israel continue the practice of celebrating an extra day for Passover and other festivals.

Jews in the United States assume that the observance and celebration of Passover today follows much the same pattern all over the world. Because American Jewish origins are predominantly Central and Eastern European, where Passover customs vary only slightly from country to country, the assumption is understandable. However, while the basic elements remain the same all over the world, the customs surrounding the observance of the holiday differ.

In the Caucasus, in the southwestern part of Russia, the Passover Seder is not celebrated in individual homes. Instead, after synagogue services, the women take the symbolic foods, as well as the prepared dinners for their families, to the home of their Hakham (learned man). Because few of them know Hebrew, it is the custom in this region for many families to gather in the house of a learned man who is able to explain the Haggadah to them. Dressed festively, everyone sits on the floor throughout the service. Their Seder is most colorful, as they act out portions of it.

At one point the Hakham wraps some matzos in a kerchief, places it on his shoulder, walks around and shows it to everyone, and explains that in this manner the Jewish people left Egypt hastily.

Later a young man from the group is costumed in torn clothes with a pack on his shoulder and a heavy stick in his hand. He goes outside the house and in a short while knocks on the door. The people ask him, without opening the door, "Who are you and what may your wish be?" Then follows a series of questions and answers to verify that he is a Jew before they will open the door and invite him to participate in the Seder. Finally they relent and greet him with great enthusiasm, asking many questions about Jerusalem, from where he supposedly arrived, and for a message concerning their liberation and redemption. He then brings them greetings, again supposedly from Jerusalem and from the sages, the towns and villages, the fields and forests, and from the holy graves. He also reports that the wise men say that there are signs pointing toward the return to the Holy City and the rebuilding of the Temple. All assembled greet this message by raising their hands high, heaving a great sigh, and repeating several times, "Amen, may thus be his will; may thus be his will."

In the neighboring countries of Syria, Iraq, Iran, and Turkey, there is much similarity to the Seder service in the Caucasus.

In Morocco the Seder also is celebrated in large groups rather than by individual family units. Here, though, it is not a matter of neighborhood or education that determines the identity of the group; it is family relationship. An entire *chamula* (Arabic for "the family together") gathers in one place. These people use two Seder symbol plates instead of one. The first is similar to the one used by Ashkenazim and the other is a bowl filled with water to hold a live fish.

The Bible says, "May you multiply like the fish in the sea." Therefore, the fish is a symbol of hope that the Jewish nation will continue to flourish.

As they begin the Haggadah, the head of the chamula takes the first symbolic Seder plate and circles it three times over the head of each person at the table and says, "In a hurry the Jews went out from Egypt."

After the Seder each one takes a piece of the Afikoman to carry with him all year as protection against evil. As in the Caucasus and nearby countries, the leader places a bag of matzos on his shoulder, this time hanging from a stick, and everyone marches out of the house singing, "This is the way our parents left Egypt. The dough was not sour and therefore we eat matzos."

On the last day of Passover it is the custom in Morocco for the Jews to eat only dairy foods. In the streets of the Jewish quarters they put out tables laden with milk, vegetables, butter, and sweet dishes so that all may partake. They greet each other on this day with wishes for a happy, good, and green year.

In Yemen the customs are much like those of the Caucasus, with a few variations. They leave the doors of their homes open all night because they believe that there is divine protection on this night. Also, they believe that when Mashiach (the Messiah) comes, it will be on a Seder night, and they leave the door open so that they can exit quickly as soon as he sounds the shofar (ram's horn).

Instead of having the Four Questions asked by one child, the Yemenites have all the children ask them. Then each gets a present from his mother—perhaps a hard-cooked egg and an extra piece of meat.

There have been countless times since the Diaspora when Jews have been forced to conceal their celebration of Passover from the Gentile world, and this was especially necessary during the Middle Ages. Wild rumors circulated about obscene and deadly rites supposedly conducted at the Seders. Ignorance and prejudice frequently found an outlet in unbelievable cruelty and violence against Jews who were doing nothing more than celebrating a quiet and joyous religious festival. A not very subtle form of persecution at various times in history has been the prohibition against baking matzos (unleavened bread) for Pesach. This fundamental food is essential for the celebration of Passover, which commemorated the haste with which the Jews left Egypt. Unable to leaven their bread before fleeing, the escapees baked dough in the sun and thus produced matzos. Naturally, to be forbidden to bake matzos or hold Jewish religious services forced some temporary adjustments in the Passover celebration. But with determination and ingenuity Jews have managed to celebrate Passover to one degree or another no matter what the obstacles.

PREPARING THE HOUSE

In the days preceding Passover, the Jewish home is the scene of frantic but joyous activity. Mama screams directions, Papa moans and groans, children complain about being overworked, and all for good reason. The house is being turned inside out. Everything is scoured, boiled, soaked, scrubbed, brushed, dusted, shined, vacuumed, scalded, burned out, or purged. Closets are emptied, washed, and relined. Curtains, draperies, and bedspreads are replaced with fresh ones. Finally, all is bright and immaculate—ready to greet this festive season.

On the night before Passover, when all is in order, the family acts out the ancient custom of "searching for the chometz" (leavened bread). Small pieces of bread have been placed strategically throughout the home. The father, accompanied by the family, "searches" for the symbolic pieces of bread, which must be removed from the home before the holiday begins. He uses a feather to brush the chometz into a wooden spoon, and his way is lit by a candle. A special prayer is recited. Not one crumb can be left.

The next morning the bustling and rushing often reach a point bordering on hysteria. Still so much to do and so little time left! After breakfast, the last of the chometzdige dishes (used during the rest of the year), glassware, pots, and silver must be removed. Out of the basement, attic, or special closets come the Passover dishes, silver, pots, glassware. At last all is in order. Preparations for the Seder meal begin.

Because it is beyond reasonable expectations to shop for Passover groceries on this last morning before Pesach, most people purchase food supplies in advance but store them in a special place where there is no chance that they will be contaminated with chometz. Now it is time to transfer them to the kitchen, where the chopping, beating, mixing, folding, boiling, simmering, roasting, and baking soon fill the home with nostalgic aromas.

While the younger children are shooed off to bed, hopefully to nap so that they can stay awake through the Seder, the rest of the family is occupied with familiar chores. It is time to set the table—the excitement intensifies.

HOW TO SET A PASSOVER SEDER TABLE

Because Passover is the holiday when Jews celebrate their liberation from slavery in Egypt, they treat themselves like royalty during the festival. Homes are spotless after the ambitious spring cleaning; clothes are the most beautiful they own; the food and wines are the best they can buy. The table, being the center of the Seder festivities, reflects the spirit of the joyous occasion. It is covered with a lovely rich cloth. The china, silverware, and glassware sparkle and gleam. Fragrant flowers and leaves form a colorful centerpiece.

With this gracious background, the picture is completed with the traditional Seder symbols. At the head of the table, where a place has been set for the father of the family, the essential foods for the ceremony are arranged:

1. Three matzos, each wrapped separately, are placed on top of each other on a plate. A portion of the middle matzo will later be put away to be used as the Afikoman (symbolic end of the meal). Matzo covers of exquisite materials are used in many homes. They have pockets for the three pieces of matzo and are usually ornately decorated. A dish of salt should be nearby, ready for sprinkling on the matzo before eating, after the blessing is made.

2. There are five symbolic foods, which should also be placed near the head of the family: lamb shankbone (Zeroa), roasted, the symbol of the Paschal lamb that in ancient times was sacrificed in the Temple; roasted egg, which is a token of grief for the destruction of the Temple; bitter herbs (Moror), which can be any variety, but usually is horseradish, and serves as a reminder of the bitterness of slavery; Charosis, a mixture of fruit, nuts, cinnamon or ginger, and sweet wine, which symbolizes the mortar made to hold together the bricks that the Jews produced while in Egyptian slavery; Karpas, which may be celery, parsley, or potatoes, and is intended to stimulate the curiosity of the children, along with a dish of salt water, because the Karpas is dipped in brine before eating as a symbol of the tears of the Jews in Egypt.

3. Candlesticks with candles are placed on the table, ready for lighting and blessing by the mother of the family.

4. A Haggadah (book of prayers and Passover stories) is put at each place setting.

5. A wine cup or glass should be placed on the table for each person and a saucer used under it to hold the "maches," the drops of wine that represent the plagues.

6. The Cup of Elijah is usually the most beautiful wine goblet in the home, often made of precious metals and sometimes set with jewels. The Prophets promised that Elijah would announce the coming of the Messiah and bring peace and freedom. Should he come on Passover night, the welcoming wine cup is made ready.

7. Eating eggs and salt water is traditional just before the Seder meal.

8. The table, of course, will have a plate of matzos and bottles of wine.

9. After the meal is served, the dessert dishes should be removed and the table cleared of relish plates and other traces of the meal. Wine must be left, however, since there are two more cups to be filled. Matzo also remains until the end of the Seder.

For a novice preparing a Seder, it is worthwhile to detail the order of service. After the company is assembled at the table, Kiddush (wine blessing) is recited. Because the head of the house must wash his hands at the table in preparation for eating the Karpas, water in a pitcher or glass, a bowl to catch the water, and a towel should be placed nearby. After the Karpas, dipped in salt water, is eaten, the Afikoman is hidden. The second cup of wine is filled, and now the big moment arrives: the youngest child asks the Four Questions about the unusual foods and procedures for the Seder. The answers, from the Haggadah service, follow. Impromptu questions are encouraged.

Hands are washed again; grace is said for the matzo; tiny sandwiches of matzo and moror are eaten. It is time to serve the Seder meal. If a child has absconded with the Afikoman (only Scrooge would prevent this theft), it must of course be redeemed, because the Seder cannot continue until the Afikoman has been consumed. Only then the grace for after meals can be recited, and the blessing said over the third cup of wine. The door of the house is opened for Elijah the Prophet; a special prayer is recited; the gentle and melodious "Eliyohu Hanavi" is sung.

After completing the Hallel (psalms of praise) and drinking the fourth cup of wine, the Seder is closed with the singing of selected Hebrew folk songs until the children are bleary-eyed and adults are hoarse.

MENU PLANNING

How many times have you heard, "Passover isn't kept the way it's supposed to be anymore," or "If this continues, we'll be buying everything for Pesach"? Of course neither of these statements is valid, but perhaps an explanation is in order.

In the shtetlach (small towns) of Europe and in the many ghettos of the world where Jews were segregated during the almost two-thousand-year Diaspora, keeping a kosher home was an exercise in self-discipline and devotion. To keep the food regulations of Passover in these alien surroundings has been even more difficult. The byword has always been, "When in doubt, don't use it." Thus, until very recent times the observant homemaker was forced to forgo many foods that might have brightened her menus. To be sure that no food contained chometz, she limited her selection to simple basic foods, the origins of which were beyond doubt. However, even some very simple foods like milk, butter, and cheese were proscribed years ago because one could not be sure of the circumstances under which they had been produced.

Today it is possible to have Rabbinical supervision over many Passover foods. The homemaker can choose from a resplendent variety of products providing not only traditional dishes like ready-to-serve gefilte fish, borscht, soups, and matzos, but also an array of cake mixes, prepared cakes and cookies, pareve margarine, catsup, mayonnaise, cranberry sauce, potato-pancake mix, pickles, processed herring products, canned fish like salmon and tuna, ice cream and sherbet, candies, potato chips, and many others. (For a detailed listing of foods available, see pages 12-14.)

So do not let yourself be shaken and doubtful when you hear, "Passover isn't kept the way it's supposed to be anymore." Passover is not a sacrifice—it is a celebration. And the meals served should reflect the festive mood. The one special food prohibition for Passover is against chometz. Take advantage of the food variety at your disposal, use imagination in planning menus, and follow the same rules of good nutrition that apply during the rest of the year.

Never serve the same food more than once in a meal. If you plan tomato juice as an appetizer, do not use tomato sauce on the meat. A well-constructed meal should have variety in texture, flavor, color, and temperature. Also, the cooking method should show some creativity. A meal in which everything is baked, or broiled, or boiled, or fried is dull and uninteresting.

The following menus are planned for those on a normal diet. They are meant merely as a guide, because you are the only one who knows the food preferences of your family, the capacity of your refrigerator and freezer, the size of your oven and stove, and the number of utensils and dishes you have. Just remember, on Passover, the head of the house is a king, his wife is a queen, and the children princes and princesses. Treat them and yourself accordingly.

1.

Wine for Kiddush

Gefilte Fish   Horseradish

Chicken Soup* with Fluffy Matzo Balls*

Turkey   Giblet Stuffing*

Brussels Sprouts   Cranberry Sauce

Tossed Lettuce and Tomatoes*

Sweet-Potato-and-Applesauce Pudding*

Matzos   Kosher Pickles

Toasted Almond Sponge Cake*

Pears Concord*

Tea   Black Coffee

SEDER SUGGESTIONS

2.

Wine for Kiddush

Fishlet Cocktail with Horseradish Sauce*

Hot Borscht   Toasted Matzo Farfel*

Capon   Parsley Stuffing*

Matzo Kugel*

Broccoli with Velvet Vegetable Sauce*

Carrot-and-Raisin Salad*

Dill Tomatoes   Almond-Cranberry Sauce*

Matzos

Chiffon Cake*   Spicy Fruit Sauce*

Tea   Black Coffee

*Recipes are given in this book for those dishes marked with asterisks.

3.
Wine for Kiddush

Chopped Liver*   Sliced Tomato

Chicken Soup* with Matzo Balls*

Smothered Chicken*

Piquant Carrots*   Potato Kugelach*

Deluxe Delight

Matzos

Lemon-Meringue Pie*

Tea   Black Coffee

SEDER SUGGESTIONS

4.
Wine for Kiddush

Whitefish and Pike with Horseradish

Chicken Soup*   Passover Mandlen*

Honeyed Duck* with Orange Sauce*

Crusty Roasted Potatoes*

Asparagus Tips

Mixed Vegetable Salad

Matzos

Fruit Meringues*

Kichelettes

Tea   Black Coffee

5.

Wine for Kiddush

Sautéed Chicken Livers* in Puff Shells*

Hot Borscht

Pot-Roasted Stuffed Chicken*

Honeyed Sweet Potatoes*

New Orleans Cauliflower*

Cranberry-Apple Relish*

Tossed Green Salad

Matzos   Kosher Dill Pickles

Six-Egg Sponge Cake* with Dessert Wine Sauce*

Tea   Black Coffee

SEDER SUGGESTIONS

6.

Wine for Kiddush

Fishlets in Tomato Flower Cups*

Chicken Soup* with Matzo Balls*

Turkey   Mushroom Stuffing*

Cranberry-Glazed Sweet Potatoes*

Spring Garden Vegetables*

Lettuce Wedge   Russian Dressing*

Matzos

Spice-Nut Sponge Cake*   Fruit Compote

Tea   Black Coffee

PASSOVER   29

BREAKFASTS

1.
Chilled Grapefruit Sections
Matzo Brei*
Coffee   Milk

2.
Apple Juice
Cream-Cheese Scrambled Eggs*
Passover Muffins*   Butter
Strawberry Preserves
Coffee   Milk

3.
Prune Juice
Soft-Cooked Eggs
Passover Bagel*   Cream Cheese
Orange Marmalade
Coffee   Milk

4.
Chilled Melon
Matzo-Meal Latkes*
Honey   Preserves
Coffee   Milk

5.
Chilled Orange Sections
Passover Cereal with Raisins
Matzos   Butter
Raspberry Preserves
Coffee   Milk

BREAKFASTS

6.
Fresh Grapefruit Juice
Creamy Marmalade Omelet*
Passover Rolls*   Butter
Coffee   Milk

7.
Prunes with Sweet Cream
Hard-Cooked Eggs
Assorted Cheeses   Pickled Herring
Matzos   Butter   Preserves
Coffee   Milk

8.
Chilled Grapefruit Sections
Griddle Cakes (made with a mix)
Hot Buttered Honey
Coffee   Milk

9.
Grape Juice
Matzo-Meal Omelet*
Matzos   Butter
Cherry Preserves
Coffee   Milk

10.
Orange Juice
Apple Fritters*   Sour Cream
Coffee   Milk

PASSOVER

LUNCHEONS OR SUPPERS

1. Turkey Blintzes with Hot Cranberry Sauce*
Tossed Green Salad
Macaroons   Fresh Fruit
Tea   Black Coffee

2. Denver Sandwiches* on
Passover Rolls*
Kosher Pickles   Carrot Sticks
Fudge Brownies*
Tea   Black Coffee

3. Schav with Sour Cream
Snappy Fish Salad*
Matzos   Butter
Fancy Cookies   Fruit Cocktail
Coffee   Milk

4. Chicken à la Princess*
on Potato Latkes*
Grapefruit, Orange, and Avocado Salad
Matzos
Mandel Cuts   Kichel
Tea   Black Coffee

5. Borscht with Sour Cream
Simple Salmon Casserole*
Creamed Spinach*
Matzos   Butter
Rozinkes Mit Mandlen Cake*
Coffee   Milk

PASSOVER

LUNCHEONS OR SUPPERS

6.
Neptune Egg Scramble*
Mashed Potatoes   Buttered Broccoli
Matzos   Butter
Fruit Meringue Charlotte*
Coffee   Milk

7.
Borscht Levantine*
Fisherman's Potato Pancakes*
with Sour Cream or Applesauce
Scalloped Tomatoes*
Fresh Fruit Cup
Coffee   Milk

8.
Tomato Juice
Matzo-Cheese Kugel*
Spring Fruit Salad   Mayonnaise
Assorted Cookies   Ice Cream
Coffee   Milk

9.
Potato Soup Verde*
Passover Rolls* with
Walnut-and-Egg Spread*
Sliced Tomatoes
Chocolate-Covered Macaroons
Fresh Fruit
Tea   Black Coffee

10.
Gefilte Fish Sauté with Dill Sauce*
Creole Eggplant*   Tossed Green Salad
Matzos   Butter
Gourmet Parfait*
Coffee   Milk

PASSOVER

DINNERS

1.
Canned Beef-Cabbage Soup
Stuffed Breast of Veal*
Marmalade Beets*   Oven-Roasted Potatoes
Mixed Vegetable Salad
Matzos
Marble Cake (made with a mix)
Tea   Black Coffee

2.
Chopped Egg and Onion
Fish Fillets Amandine*
Boiled New Potatoes   Sour Cream
Stewed Tomatoes
Cole Slaw
Matzos   Butter
Refrigerator Loaf Cake*
Coffee   Milk

3.
Spring Vegetable Soup*
Brisket Roast II*   Pot-Roasted Potatoes
Piquant Carrots*
Waldorf Salad*
Matzos   Kosher Pickles
Coffee Pound Cake*
Tea   Black Coffee

4.
Tomato Juice
Liver Cutlets* with Onion Sauce*
Celery and Carrots à l'Athène*
Mashed Potatoes
Deluxe Delight   Matzos
Elberta Peaches   Assorted Cookies
Tea   Black Coffee

5.
Chicken Soup* with Passover Noodles*
Creole Lamb Chops*
Potatoes en Casserole*   Broccoli
Spring Vegetable Salad
Matzos
Jelly Roll*
Tea   Black Coffee

6.
Apple Juice
Stuffed Cabbage*
Savory Matzo Farfel*
Vegetable Medley*
Celery Hearts   Dill Tomatoes
Matzos
Hermits*
Bartlett Pears
Tea   Black Coffee

DINNERS

7.
Fresh Tomato Soup*
Fruited Beef*
Fluffy Potato Knaidlach*
Asparagus
Lettuce Wedge   Mayonnaise
Matzos
Apple-Crumb Pudding*
Tea   Black Coffee

8.
Easy Chopped Herring*
Veal Sauterne*
Baked Potatoes with Pareve Margarine
Lyonnaise Carrots*
Sliced Cucumber with Vinegar and Sugar
Matzos
Banana-Nut Chiffon Cake*
Tea   Black Coffee

PASSOVER

9.
Hamishe Vegetable Soup*
Easiest-Ever Beef Loaf*
French-Fried Potatoes
Deborah's Brussels Sprouts*
Mixed Vegetable Salad
Matzos
Macaroons   Sliced Cling Peaches
Tea   Black Coffee

10.
Borscht Buttermilk Shake*
Baked Fish and Vegetables*
Special Cole Slaw*
Matzos   Butter
Strawberries-and-Cream Blintzes*
Coffee   Milk

DINNERS

APPETIZERS AND SOUPS

APPETIZERS AND SOUPS

Who ever heard of a canapé or hors d'oeuvre for Passover? Why not? All right, so matzo doesn't break evenly. People make allowances on Pesach.

In the days when the rotund figure was an object of envy and admiration, appetizers made much more sense than they do today. Their purpose is to awaken the taste buds and prepare them for the gustatory sensations to follow. In your selections, remember the purpose of this course, and serve it as attractively as you can. There are few things as repulsive as a soggy canapé. To avoid this catastrophe, do not spread the pieces of matzo or fill the hors d'oeuvre puffs until the last possible moment. In fact, it is better to put out bowls of spreads and trays of matzos and let the guests help themselves. Why should you do all the work?

APPETIZERS AND SOUPS 39

HOT FISH HORS D'OEUVRES

1-pound jar Fishlets
½ cup matzo meal
Peanut oil

Don't let the simplicity of this recipe fool you. At a party, these vanish before anything else is touched.

Heat peanut oil until hot but not smoking (375°F) in a deep, straight-sided pot (pages 106-107). Drain Fishlets and roll in matzo meal. Place in a wire basket or strainer and fry until golden brown. Serve hot on toothpicks with Horseradish Dip. Makes about 35.

HORSERADISH DIP

¼ cup mayonnaise
¼ cup red horseradish, well drained

Combine and serve with the Hot Fish Hors d'Oeuvres.

FISHLET COCKTAIL WITH HORSERADISH SAUCE

2-pound jar Fishlets, chilled
Crisp lettuce leaves
½ cup mayonnaise
½ cup red horseradish, well drained

Arrange lettuce in sherbet or coupe glasses. Place 8 to 10 Fishlets in each glass. Mix mayonnaise and horseradish. Place a generous spoonful of sauce in each glass. Serves 8 to 10.

FISHLETS IN TOMATO FLOWER CUPS

Allow one small tomato for each serving. Cut a slice from the top of each tomato. Cut the tomato almost through to the bottom into 8 petal-like sections. Separate to form flower and fill center with Fishlets. Serve on lettuce with horseradish.

EASY CHOPPED HERRING

8-ounce jar pickled herring, or herring in wine sauce
1 matzo
1 medium apple, peeled and cored
1 medium onion
1 tablespoon sugar
2 hard-cooked eggs

Remember the hours spent soaking, skinning, and boning herring? No wonder few people bothered with this meichel (treat) at home. No more. Anyone can make this successfully in no time at all.

Drain herring and save liquid. Bone pickled herring. Crush matzo and soak in the liquid from the herring. Combine and chop all ingredients except the eggs, until very fine. Chop eggs coarsely and add to herring mixture.

GEFILTE FISH

4 pounds mixed fish (carp, whitefish, and yellow pike)
3 large onions
2 eggs
2 tablespoons matzo meal
1 tablespoon salt
⅛ teaspoon pepper
½ cup water
3 large carrots, sliced
1 teaspoon salt
Dash pepper

The only way to make sure of the seasoning in homemade gefilte fish is to taste some of the fish mixture before forming it into patties. Just try to remember that the Japanese eat raw fish all the time.

Fillet the fish. Save the bones, skin, and head. Grind the filleted fish and one of the onions in a food grinder, using the fine blade. Place in a large wooden chopping bowl; add eggs, matzo meal, the 1 tablespoon salt, ⅛ teaspoon pepper, and water. Chop until smooth, soft, and light. Let stand 10 minutes. Wet hands with cold water and shape fish into oval patties. Place skin, bones, head, remaining 2 onions, sliced, and carrots in a large pot. Add the teaspoon of salt and dash of pepper. Cover with water and bring to a boil. Add fish patties carefully. Add additional water if necessary, to cover the fish. Cover the pot, bring rapidly to a boil and then simmer for about 2 hours. Juice should be reduced to about half the original volume. Allow to cool about one hour before removing fish and carrots from the pot. Strain liquid. Serve fish hot or cold with some of the liquid and horseradish. Serves 10 to 12.

NIPPY FISH CANAPÉS

1-pound jar gefilte fish
¼ cup finely chopped celery
¼ cup mayonnaise
¼ cup butter
2 tablespoons horseradish

Drain and mash fish. Add celery and mayonnaise, blending well. Combine butter and horseradish. Spread pieces of matzos with butter mixture and then with fish mixture. Or blend all ingredients and use to fill Hors d'Oeuvre Puffs (page 43).

WALNUT-AND-EGG SPREAD

4 hard-cooked eggs
¼ cup chopped walnuts
Mayonnaise
Salt and pepper

Force eggs through a coarse sieve or chop finely. Add remaining ingredients, using enough mayonnaise to bind ingredients, and season to taste. Spread mixture on pieces of matzos or use to fill Hors d'Oeuvre Puffs (page 43).

PICKLED-HERRING AND CREAM-CHEESE SPREAD

8-ounce jar pickled herring or herring in wine sauce
8 ounces cream cheese

Drain herring. Bone pickled herring. Chop the herring plus the onions from the jar. Blend with cream cheese. Chill before serving. Spread on pieces of matzos or use to fill Hors d'Oeuvre Puffs (page 43).

CRUNCHY SPREAD

Blend 4 ounces of softened cream cheese with ¼ cup blanched, chopped almonds and 1 tablespoon chopped green pepper. Spread on pieces of matzos or use to fill Hors d'Oeuvre Puffs (page 43).

GARLIC-CHEESE SPREAD

8 ounces cream cheese
¼ cup mayonnaise
¼ teaspoon garlic powder

Combine ingredients; chill. Spread on pieces of matzos or use to fill Hors d'Oeuvre Puffs (page 43).

KNISHELACH

1 medium onion, diced
3 tablespoons chicken fat or pareve margarine
½ pound liver, broiled and ground
3 cups (5 large) mashed potatoes
2 eggs, slightly beaten
2 tablespoons chicken fat or pareve margarine
1 teaspoon salt
⅛ teaspoon pepper
6 tablespoons matzo meal
1 egg yolk beaten with 1 tablespoon water

Sauté onion in the 3 tablespoons fat. Combine with ground liver and season to taste. Combine mashed potatoes with eggs, the 2 tablespoons of fat, salt, pepper, and matzo meal. Form into walnut-sized balls. Make a depression in the center of each and fill with liver mixture. Brush with diluted egg yolk. Place on a well-greased baking sheet and bake in a hot oven (400°F) 20 minutes or until well browned. Makes 3½ dozen.

SAUTÉED CHICKEN LIVERS

1 pound chicken livers
¼ cup chicken fat
2 large onions, sliced
1 pound mushrooms, sliced
1 tablespoon potato starch
10½-ounce can condensed clear chicken soup, undiluted
¼ cup sauterne wine
Salt and pepper to taste

Broil livers. Cut into bite-size pieces. Sauté onions and mushrooms in the fat until tender. Add livers; sauté 2 minutes. Mix potato starch with a few spoonfuls of the soup. Add this mixture and the balance of the soup to the livers. Stir and cook 5 minutes. Stir in wine. Season to taste. For more gravy, add additional wine. Serve in Puff Shells (page 170). Serves 6.

CHOPPED LIVER

This recipe works equally well with beef, steer, calf, or chicken liver.

Broil liver. Sauté onions in the chicken fat. Grind liver and onions in meat grinder, using fine blade, or chop by hand. Chop hard-cooked eggs and mix into liver. Season to taste with salt and pepper. Chill.

CRUNCHY CHICKEN SPREAD

1 cup minced, cooked chicken
3 tablespoons minced celery
3 tablespoons chopped nuts
Mayonnaise

Combine all ingredients, using enough mayonnaise to bind mixture. Chill. Spread on pieces of matzos or use to fill Hors d'Oeuvre Puffs (page 43).

CHICKEN SPREAD AMANDINE

1 cup finely minced chicken
3 tablespoons chicken fat
½ cup blanched almonds
½ teaspoon salt
1 tablespoon dry Concord wine

Heat chicken fat in a skillet. Add blanched almonds and toast over low heat, stirring frequently. Drain nuts and chop finely. Combine chicken fat and chopped nuts with remaining ingredients. Serve on pieces of matzos or use to fill Hors d'Oeuvre Puffs (page 43).

TANGY TONGUE CANAPÉS

2 cups minced, cooked tongue
3 tablespoons prepared horseradish
Dash garlic powder
Dash pepper
½ cup mayonnaise, approximately

Combine all ingredients. Chill. Serve on pieces of matzos or use to fill Hors d'Oeuvre Puffs (page 43).

HORS D'OEUVRE PUFFS

1 cup boiling water
⅓ cup peanut oil
½ teaspoon salt
2 teaspoons sugar
1 cup cake meal
4 eggs

In a saucepan, combine the boiling water, oil, salt, and sugar; bring to a slow boil. Reduce heat; add cake meal all at once. Stir vigorously over low heat until mixture forms a ball and leaves the sides of the pan. Remove from heat. Add unbeaten eggs one at a time, beating very thoroughly after each addition, until dough is smooth and thick. Drop by teaspoons onto well-greased cookie sheet. Bake in a hot oven (400°F) about 20 minutes or until puffed and golden brown. Do not open door to oven during early part of baking. Cool. Cut off tops. Fill as desired; replace tops. Makes 4 to 5 dozen.

SPRING VEGETABLE SOUP

2 medium potatoes, peeled
1 small zucchini squash, unpeeled
2 large carrots, scraped
1 small onion
3 scallions
2 stalks celery
3 tablespoons pareve margarine or chicken fat
2 10½-ounce cans condensed clear chicken soup
2 soup cans water
1 teaspoon sugar
Salt and pepper

Dice vegetables. In a 3-quart saucepan, sauté the vegetables in the fat for a few minutes. Add the condensed soup, water, and sugar; cover and simmer 20 minutes or until vegetables are tender. Season to taste with salt and pepper. Serves 6.

GOLDEN ONION SOUP

1½ tablespoons chicken fat
3 cups onion, sliced paper thin
2 10½-ounce cans condensed clear chicken soup
2 soup cans water

Sauté onion in chicken fat until soft and golden brown. Add condensed chicken soup and water. Bring to a boil, cover, reduce heat, and simmer for about 45 minutes. Serve with Toasted Matzo Farfel (page 49). Serves 5 or 6.

CHICKEN SOUP

1 soup chicken
3 to 4 quarts water
1 tablespoon salt
2 teaspoons sugar
1 large whole onion
2 large carrots, scraped
1 parsnip, peeled
2 stalks celery, including leaves
2 sprigs dill
4 sprigs Italian parsley

Chicken may be left whole or cut up as desired. Place it in a large kettle. Add the water, salt, and sugar. Cover and bring to a boil. Add onion, carrots, and parsnip. Tie celery, dill, and parsley together; add to pot. Cover and simmer 2 to 3 hours or until chicken is tender. Skim sediment from top of soup. Season to taste with salt and white pepper. Makes 2½ to 3 quarts.

POTATO SOUP VERDE

1½ tablespoons pareve margarine
1 large onion, diced
4 large potatoes, peeled and quartered
2 10½-ounce cans condensed clear chicken soup
5 cups water
1½ teaspoons salt
1 pound spinach, washed and chopped

Sauté onion in margarine until tender but not brown; set aside. Cook potatoes in mixture of the condensed soup, water, and salt until tender. Rice the potatoes or work through a sieve; return them to the soup. Add spinach and sautéed onions. Cook over high heat 3 minutes, stirring constantly. Do not overcook. Serves 6.

FRESH TOMATO SOUP

10½-ounce can condensed clear chicken soup, undiluted
½ bunch scallions, sliced thin
1¼ cups pared and diced cucumber
¼ cup diced green pepper
¼ cup diced celery
1½ pounds tomatoes, peeled and diced
⅔ cup tomato juice
1 tablespoon sugar
Salt and pepper

Place chicken soup, scallions, cucumber, green pepper, celery, and tomatoes in a saucepan; bring to a boil, cover, and simmer 10 minutes. Add tomato juice and sugar; cover and simmer 5 minutes more. Season to taste with salt and pepper. Serve with Toasted Matzo Farfel (page 49). Serves 4 to 6.

HAMISHE VEGETABLE SOUP

¼ cup pareve margarine or chicken fat
1½ cups thinly sliced carrots
½ cup diced onion
3 cups finely shredded cabbage
2 cups diced potatoes
1 teaspoon sugar
2 10½-ounce cans condensed clear chicken soup
2 soup cans water
Salt and pepper

Melt the fat in a large saucepan. Add the carrots, onion, cabbage, and potatoes. Cover and cook over low heat 10 minutes, stirring occasionally. Add sugar, chicken soup, and water. Bring to a boil; reduce heat and simmer 20 minutes. Season to taste with salt and pepper. Serves 6.

BORSCHT BUTTERMILK SHAKE

1-quart jar borscht, chilled
2 cups buttermilk
Minced chives

Strain borscht or mix in a blender at high speed for ½ minute. Combine thoroughly with buttermilk and chill. Serve in tall glasses garnished with a sprinkle of minced chives.

BORSCHT SHAKE

1-quart jar borscht, chilled
¾ cup heavy sour cream

Strain the borscht. Add cream and whip thoroughly with egg beater, electric mixer, or blender. Serve in tall, chilled glasses.

BORSCHT FROST

Chill and strain a 1-quart jar of borscht. Place the liquid, plus 2 raw eggs, in a closely sealed jar. Shake vigorously until frothy. Or combine in a blender at high speed for ½ minute. Serve in tall, chilled glasses.

BORSCHT LEVANTINE

1-quart jar borscht
2 cups yogurt

Strain borscht or mix in a blender at high speed for ½ minute. Add yogurt and stir thoroughly. Chill and serve in tall glasses.

BORSCHT BISQUE

2 cups (4 large) mashed potatoes
¼ teaspoon onion powder
¾ teaspoon salt
¾ cup sour cream
1-quart jar borscht, strained

Combine potatoes, onion powder, salt, and sour cream. Gradually stir in borscht; chill and serve. If a blender is available, do not strain borscht. Blend all ingredients at high speed for ½ minute, using only half the ingredients at a time if the blender jar is not large enough. Serves 4 to 6.

SOUP ACCESSORIES

Why four different matzo-ball recipes? Well, fifty still would not cover all the variations. So here are four general types, each the best in that category. When people discuss matzo balls, they usually rhapsodize about their lightness and delicacy. However, when pressed, many people will admit, if a little shamefacedly, that they were accustomed to firm matzo balls at home and still prefer them.

There is a widespread myth about knaidlach that should be dispelled once and for all. Seltzer will not make matzo balls any lighter than water does. Perhaps it is the bubbles that convinced so many women that seltzer would cause more lightness. This is not so, because the seltzer bubbles collapse once they are mixed with the other ingredients.

FIRM MATZO BALLS

1 cup matzo meal
½ teaspoon salt
3 tablespoons fat
2 eggs, well beaten
½ cup water, approximately

Blend matzo meal with salt, fat, and well-beaten eggs. Mix thoroughly. Add sufficient cold water to make a dough heavy enough to be shaped into balls. Cook in covered kettle of boiling salted water or boiling soup for 15 minutes. Makes 12.

TRADITIONAL MATZO BALLS

2 tablespoons fat
2 eggs, slightly beaten
½ cup matzo meal
1 teaspoon salt
2 tablespoons soup stock or water

Mix fat and eggs together. Mix and add matzo meal and salt. When well blended, add soup stock or water. Cover mixing bowl and place in refrigerator for at least 20 minutes. Using a 3-quart pot, bring salted water to a brisk boil. Reduce flame and into the slightly bubbling water drop balls formed from above mixture. Cover pot and let cook 30 to 40 minutes. Have soup at room temperature or warmer and remove matzo balls from water to soup pot. When ready to serve, allow soup to simmer for about five minutes. Recipe makes 8 balls.

FLUFFY MATZO BALLS

3 eggs, separated
¾ cup matzo meal
½ teaspoon salt

Beat egg whites until stiff; then fold in yolks, which have been beaten with the salt. Fold in matzo meal. Let stand five minutes; then form balls with a spoon and drop into boiling soup stock or salt water. Cover and cook 35 minutes. Recipe makes 12 large balls.

ECONOMY MATZO BALLS

1 cup matzo meal
1 cup boiling water
2 tablespoons melted fat or oil
1 egg, well beaten
1 teaspoon salt
Dash white pepper
2 tablespoons chopped parsley (optional)

Combine matzo meal and boiling water thoroughly. Add fat, egg, salt, pepper, and parsley. Mix well and place in refrigerator for about one-half hour. With hands wet in cold water, make balls about 1 inch in diameter. Drop into gently boiling water. Cover and cook for 25 minutes. Serve in hot soup. Makes 16.

PASSOVER MANDLEN

¼ cup peanut oil
6 tablespoons water
½ teaspoon salt
Pinch pepper
1 cup matzo meal
2 eggs

Place in a saucepan and bring to a boil the oil, water, salt, and pepper. Add the matzo meal and blend over low heat until mixture forms a ball and pulls away from the side of the pan. Remove from the heat and cool slightly. Beat in the eggs, one at a time, until the dough is smooth. With lightly oiled hands, shape the dough into tiny balls. Place on a well-oiled baking sheet and bake in a hot oven (400°F) 30 minutes or until golden brown. Serve in hot chicken soup. Or delicious as a snack. Makes 4 to 5 dozen.

TOASTED MATZO FARFEL

2 cups matzo farfel
2 eggs, beaten
¼ teaspoon salt

Combine the matzo farfel with the egg and salt. Spread in a thin layer on a greased baking pan. Bake in a moderate oven (350°F) 20 to 25 minutes or until lightly browned. Serve in your favorite soup.

FLUFFY POTATO KNAIDLACH

1 egg
1 cup cold water
3-ounce package potato-pancake mix
¼ cup matzo meal
2 tablespoons oil or melted fat

Beat egg with a fork; blend in the water. Add remaining ingredients; stir; allow to thicken 10 minutes. Form into balls the size of a walnut. Drop into a large pot of rapidly boiling salted water. Cover tightly, reduce heat, and simmer 30 minutes. Drain and serve in soup, stew, or as a side dish with meats and poultry. Makes 15 to 18.

PASSOVER NOODLES

3 eggs
3 tablespoons water
¼ teaspoon salt
3 tablespoons cake meal
Peanut oil

Beat eggs lightly; beat in water, salt, and cake meal until smooth. Grease a 9-inch skillet with peanut oil and heat until a drop of water sizzles when dropped on the pan. Pour 3 tablespoons of batter onto the pan and rotate until batter covers entire bottom of pan. Cook over moderate heat until lightly browned; turn and brown other side. Do not overcook or it will be too crisp to handle. Turn out of pan. Repeat until all the batter is used, greasing skillet each time. Roll up each pancake and slice into thin strips. Put into boiling soup for a minute or two before serving.

MEATS

MEATS

No doubt, when you have taken recipes from general cookbooks and adapted them to fit the regulations of Kashruth, you have found them too salty. When meat is koshered, it retains some of the sprinkling salt. These recipes were prepared, of course, with koshered meats, but they were all very well rinsed. If you have any question about how salty your meat or poultry is to start with, cut down on the salt in the recipes. You can always add more later. Should you find that a soup, stew, or any dish with gravy is too salty, cut a potato in quarters and cook it in the pot for a while. It will absorb some of the salt.

MEATS 53

BRISKET ROAST I

4 pounds brisket of beef
1 large onion, sliced
¼ cup chopped green pepper
½ cup chopped celery
11-ounce can tomato-and-mushroom sauce
1 teaspoon salt
¼ teaspoon pepper
6 medium potatoes, peeled

Brown meat in a Dutch oven. If meat is very lean, use a little fat for browning. Add sliced onion, green pepper, and celery; sauté until tender. Add tomato-and-mushroom sauce, salt, and pepper. Cover and simmer 2½ to 3 hours or until tender. Cut potatoes in half and add during last half-hour of cooking. If desired, this may be roasted in a moderate oven (350°F) for the same length of time. Serves 6 to 8.

BRISKET ROAST II

4 pounds brisket of beef
3 tablespoons cake meal
1 teaspoon salt
¼ teaspoon pepper
¼ teaspoon garlic powder
2 cups cooked or canned tomatoes
2 medium onions, sliced
1 small green pepper, diced
½ cup diced celery

Brown meat slowly in a heavy roasting pan or Dutch oven. If it is very lean, add a little fat. Combine cake meal, salt, pepper, and garlic powder. Sprinkle over meat. Add tomatoes, onions, green pepper, and celery. Cover pan and roast in a moderate oven (350°F) for about 3 hours or until tender, or cook over low heat on top of the stove for the same length of time. Add water if necessary. If desired, cook potatoes with the meat during the last hour, adding extra salt if you do this. Serves 8.

DEBORAH'S STEAK ROLL-UPS

3 pounds shoulder steak, cut ¼ inch thick
1 medium onion, minced
2 tablespoons shortening or chicken fat
3 matzos,* coarsely broken
¼ teaspoon pepper
1 teaspoon salt
6 tablespoons hot water
½ cup cake meal or matzo meal
11-ounce can tomato-and-mushroom sauce
¼ cup water

Cut meat into 6 to 8 portions. Sauté onion in shortening. Combine with broken matzos, pepper, salt, and hot water. Pound meat very thin with a mallet or side of a heavy plate. Place a spoonful of stuffing in the center of each piece of meat. Roll up and fasten with toothpicks, skewers, or string. Roll in the cake meal or matzo meal. Brown in a small amount of fat in a skillet. Add tomato-and-mushroom sauce plus water; cover and simmer about one hour or until tender. Serves 6 to 8.

*1¾ cups matzo farfel may be used instead.

SAVORY CHUCK STEAK

3 pounds chuck steak, cut 2 inches thick
¼ cup matzo meal
1 small green pepper, diced
2 medium onions, sliced
1½ teaspoons salt
¼ teaspoon pepper
11-ounce can tomato-and-mushroom sauce
¼ cup water

Dredge meat with matzo meal. Brown on both sides in a small amount of fat, using a large heavy pan. Add remaining ingredients. Cover and simmer 2½ hours or until tender. Serves 6 to 8.

COUNTRY-FRIED SHOULDER STEAKS

1½ pounds shoulder steak, ½ inch thick
2 eggs, beaten
2 tablespoons water
¾ cup matzo meal
3 tablespoons vegetable shortening
Salt and pepper

Pound steak thoroughly with meat pounder or side of heavy saucer. Cut into serving pieces. Mix eggs and water. Dip meat in matzo meal, then in egg mixture, and again in matzo meal. Brown on both sides in hot fat. Season with salt and pepper. Cover and cook over very low heat 20 minutes or until tender. Serves 4.

FRUITED BEEF WITH FLUFFY POTATO KNAIDLACH

2 pounds boneless chuck, cut in 1½-inch cubes
⅓ cup matzo meal or cake meal
½ teaspoon salt
¼ teaspoon pepper
¼ cup peanut oil
2 cloves garlic, minced
1 large onion, chopped
1 can (2½ cups) tomato juice
2 cups sliced carrots
1 cup sliced celery
1 medium green pepper, diced
1 large apple, peeled, cored, and diced
1-pound jar fruit compote
½ teaspoon cinnamon
½ teaspoon ginger

Roll meat in mixture of meal, salt, and pepper. Brown in the hot oil in a large saucepan or Dutch oven. Add garlic and onion; cook until onion is tender. Add liquid from the jar of fruit compote and the tomato juice; cover and simmer about 1 hour or until meat is almost tender. Add vegetables and cook about 10 minutes longer. Remove prune pits and cut fruit compote into bite-size pieces. Add to meat, along with apple, cinnamon, and ginger; cook 10 minutes longer or until tender. Serve with Fluffy Potato Knaidlach (page 50). Serves 4 to 6.

BEEF IN RED WINE

2 pounds lean boneless chuck, cut into 2-inch cubes
1 cup medium-dry Concord wine
½ cup matzo meal or cake meal
½ teaspoon salt
⅛ teaspoon pepper
¼ cup oil or vegetable shortening
1½ cups boiling water
1 pound carrots, sliced
1 pound small white onions
1 teaspoon salt

Place meat in a bowl; pour wine over it; cover and refrigerate several hours or overnight. Drain and save wine. Roll meat in mixture of the meal, salt, and pepper. In a Dutch oven, brown meat in the hot fat. Stir in boiling water and half the wine. Cover and simmer 2 hours or until almost tender. Add balance of wine, carrots, onions, and salt. Cover and simmer 45 minutes or until tender. Serves 6.

BEEF PAPRIKA

2 pounds lean beef, cut in cubes
2 medium onions, sliced
2 tablespoons fat
½ teaspoon salt
¼ teaspoon pepper
¼ teaspoon garlic powder
½ cup boiling water
¾ cup chopped green pepper
1 cup chopped celery
1 tablespoon paprika
½ cup cooked or canned peeled tomatoes

Brown meat and onions in the fat in a heavy 4-quart saucepan; add salt, pepper, garlic powder, water, green pepper, celery, paprika, and tomatoes. Cover and simmer until tender, about two hours. Stir occasionally and add more water if necessary. Serves 6.

POT ROAST MARINADE

4 pounds beef pot roast
1½ cups sliced onion
1 cup diced celery
1½ teaspoons salt
⅛ teaspoon pepper
6 sprigs parsley
1½ cups medium-dry Concord wine
¼ cup cake meal
¼ teaspoon salt
Dash pepper

About 18 to 24 hours before cooking, marinate the beef in a mixture of the next 6 ingredients. Cover and place in a refrigerator. Turn occasionally. Just before cooking, remove meat and rub it with a mixture of the cake meal, salt, and pepper. Brown meat in a small amount of fat. Add wine mixture. Cover pot and simmer slowly until tender, about 3 hours, basting occasionally. Add a little water if the liquid boils dry. Serves 6 to 8.

TZIMMES WITH HALKE

2 pounds brisket of beef
1 large onion, diced
1 pound carrots, sliced
3 medium sweet potatoes, sliced
2 tablespoons cake meal
1½ teaspoons salt
¼ teaspoon pepper
½ cup sugar

Place beef and diced onion in a covered saucepan and cover with water. Cook one hour. Add carrots and cook one-half hour longer. Make the Halke (see recipe below) and place in a Dutch oven or small covered roasting pan. Place meat and carrots in the pan, saving the liquid to make gravy. Add the sweet-potato slices to the roasting pan. Skim the fat off the liquid. If this liquid does not measure 2 cups, add water. Put the cake meal, salt, and pepper into the pot in which the meat was boiled. Gradually stir in the liquid, stirring well to prevent lumps. Cook over moderate heat, stirring constantly, until thickened. Add the sugar and mix thoroughly. Pour over tzimmes and halke. Cover and bake in a moderate oven (350°F) for one hour. Uncover and bake one-half hour longer.

HALKE

1½ cups very well-drained potato (it should be almost dry)
1 egg, beaten
Dash pepper
¼ teaspoon salt
2 tablespoons grated onion
1 tablespoon chicken fat
½ cup matzo meal (approximately)

Combine all ingredients, adding as much matzo meal as necessary to make a dough which can be shaped into a ball. With lightly greased hands, shape entire mixture into a large oval or a ball. Place in pan which will be used to roast the tzimmes.

SWISS STEAK

2 pounds lean boneless chuck or beef shoulder, about 1½ inches thick
⅓ cup matzo meal
1 large onion, diced
11-ounce can tomato-and-mushroom sauce
½ cup water

Pound matzo meal into meat with a wooden potato masher or the edge of a heavy plate. Brown meat on all sides in a little fat in a heavy skillet or Dutch oven. Add onion, tomato-and-mushroom sauce, and water. Cover and simmer 1½ hours or until meat is very tender. Serves 5 or 6.

EASIEST-EVER BEEF LOAF

2 pounds ground beef
2 eggs, slightly beaten
3-ounce package potato-pancake mix
½ cup water
11-ounce can tomato-and-mushroom sauce

Combine all ingredients except ½ cup of the tomato-and-mushroom sauce. Pack into a greased 9×5×3-inch loaf pan or shape into a loaf in a greased shallow pan. Top with remaining sauce. Bake in a moderate oven (350°F) one hour. Serves 6 to 8.

HIDDEN-TREASURE MEAT LOAF

2 pounds ground chuck
2 eggs, slightly beaten
¾ cup matzo meal
½ teaspoon salt
⅛ teaspoon pepper
11-ounce can tomato-and-mushroom sauce
6 (about ¾ pound) frankfurters

Mix beef with eggs, matzo meal, salt, pepper, and ½ cup tomato-and-mushroom sauce. Pack half this mixture into a greased 9×5×3-inch loaf pan or shape in a greased shallow pan. Arrange four frankfurters lengthwise on the meat; cut the remaining two in half and arrange lengthwise also, so that frankfurters cover the entire length of the meat. Top with the balance of the meat mixture. Pour the rest of the tomato and mushroom sauce over the top. Bake in a moderate oven (350°F) one hour. Serves 8.

APPLESAUCE MEAT LOAF

2 pounds ground beef
1 cup applesauce
½ teaspoon salt
¼ teaspoon pepper
2 eggs, slightly beaten
¾ cup matzo meal
11-ounce can tomato-and-mushroom sauce

Combine all ingredients, except ½ cup of the tomato-and-mushroom sauce. Pack into a greased 9×5×3-inch loaf pan or shape into a loaf in a greased shallow pan. Top with remaining tomato-and-mushroom sauce. Bake in a moderate oven (350°F) for one hour. Serves 6 to 8.

JIFFY MEAT LOAF

2 pounds ground beef
1 teaspoon salt
¼ teaspoon pepper
2 eggs, slightly beaten
¾ cup matzo meal
¼ cup tomato juice
¼ cup catsup
½ cup finely minced onion

This recipe is perfect for the days when you want to make meat loaf but don't have time to bake one for an hour.

Combine all ingredients and mix well. Form into a rectangular loaf, one inch thick, on a shallow pan. Broil, four to five inches away from the broiler unit, 10 to 15 minutes, without turning. Serves 6 to 8.

FROSTED BEEF LOAF

2 pounds ground beef
¾ cup matzo meal
½ cup canned tomato-and-mushroom sauce
2 eggs, slightly beaten
½ cup minced onion
1 teaspoon salt
¼ teaspoon pepper
3 pounds (9 medium) potatoes, cooked
5 tablespoons chicken fat
⅓ cup canned condensed clear chicken soup, heated
½ teaspoon salt
⅛ teaspoon pepper

Combine ground beef with next 6 ingredients. Pack into a well-greased loaf pan and bake in a moderate oven (350°F) for one hour. Unmold onto a baking sheet or heat-proof platter. Mash potatoes and whip with fat, soup, and seasonings. Spread top and sides of beef loaf with this mixture. Brush lightly with chicken fat and place in a moderate oven for 15 to 20 minutes or until lightly browned. Serves 6 to 8.

PINWHEEL MEAT LOAF

2 pounds ground beef
1 teaspoon salt
¼ teaspoon pepper
2 eggs
¾ cup matzo meal
¼ cup tomato juice
2 matzos, finely broken*
3 tablespoons minced onion
3 tablespoons melted chicken fat
½ teaspoon salt
Dash pepper
⅓ cup hot water
½ cup canned tomato-and-mushroom sauce

Combine ground beef with the next 5 ingredients. Combine broken matzo or farfel with the next 5 ingredients to make filling. Place meat mixture between 2 sheets of waxed paper and press or roll out into a one-half-inch-thick rectangle. Remove top sheet of paper and spread the meat surface with the filling mixture. Roll firmly, jelly-roll fashion, using the waxed paper to help guide the meat. Place in a greased, shallow baking pan; cover with the tomato-and-mushroom sauce. Bake in a moderate oven (350°F) one hour. Serves 6 to 8.

*1½ cups matzo farfel may be used instead.

SWEET-AND-SOUR MEAT LOAF

2 pounds ground beef
1 medium onion
1 cup crushed matzos*
¾ teaspoon salt
⅛ teaspoon pepper
½ cup water
2 eggs, beaten
11-ounce can tomato-and-mushroom sauce
¼ cup lemon juice
½ cup sugar

Combine and mix well the meat, onion, matzo crumbs, salt, pepper, water, eggs, and ½ cup of the tomato-and-mushroom sauce. In a greased baking dish, shape into a loaf. Combine remaining tomato-and-mushroom sauce, lemon juice, and sugar. Pour over meat. Bake in moderate oven (350°F) one hour, basting frequently. Serves 6.

*1 cup matzo farfel may be used instead.

SURPRISE MEAT LOAF

¼ cup pareve margarine, melted
½ cup minced onion
3 egg matzos, finely broken
2 tablespoons minced parsley
1 egg, beaten
2 tablespoons water
2 pounds ground chuck
½ teaspoon salt
¼ teaspoon pepper
2 eggs, beaten
¾ cup matzo meal
11-ounce can tomato-and-mushroom sauce

Combine first 6 ingredients and set aside. Combine remaining 6 ingredients except for ½ cup of the tomato-and-mushroom sauce. Pack half the meat into a greased 9×5×3-inch loaf pan. Add matzo mixture and then the remaining meat. Pour remaining tomato-and-mushroom sauce over the top. Bake in a moderate oven (350°F) 1¼ hours. Serves 6 to 8.

HOLIDAY BEEF RING

2 pounds ground beef
¾ cup matzo meal
½ cup canned tomato-and-mushroom sauce
2 eggs, slightly beaten
½ cup minced onion
1 teaspoon salt
¼ teaspoon pepper

Combine all ingredients thoroughly. Pack into a well-greased 6-cup ring mold. (For extra ease in removal after baking, the mold may be lined with cheesecloth which has been oiled.) Bake in a moderate oven (350°F) for 45 minutes. Unmold on a large platter. Fill center with cooked and seasoned vegetables and surround with parsley potatoes. Serve with heated canned tomato-and-mushroom sauce. Serves 6.

SURPRISE KLOPS

2 pounds ground beef
2 eggs, slightly beaten
¾ cup matzo meal
1 teaspoon salt
⅛ teaspoon pepper
¼ cup tomato juice
6 to 8 hard-cooked eggs
11-ounce can tomato-and-mushroom sauce
¾ cup water
1 large onion, minced
⅛ teaspoon garlic powder

Mix meat with beaten eggs, matzo meal, salt, pepper, and tomato juice. Divide into 6 to 8 portions. Shape each portion around an unsliced hard-cooked egg to form a large meatball. Place in a large saucepan; add tomato-and-mushroom sauce, water, onion, and garlic powder. Cover and simmer about one hour. If desired, these may be baked in the oven at 350°F for about one hour. Serves 6 to 8.

CHICKEN-GIBLET FRICASSEE

Giblets from 2 chickens (feet, hearts, gizzards, and necks)
3 medium onions, diced
2 pounds ground beef
2 eggs, slightly beaten
2 matzos, finely broken
⅔ cup cold water
2 teaspoons salt
¼ teaspoon pepper
2 teaspoons paprika

Scald chicken feet with boiling water and pull off skin. Cut giblets into small pieces. Add diced onion and cover with water. Cover and simmer until tender, about 1½ to 2 hours. Soak broken matzos in cold water. Combine with ground beef and beaten eggs. Shape into small meatballs and drop into hot giblet mixture. Add seasonings, cover, and cook gently for at least one-half hour. Longer cooking gives a superior blend of flavors. Serves 4 to 6.

SAUCY MEATBALLS

2 pounds ground beef
¾ cup matzo meal
½ cup water
2 eggs, slightly beaten
½ cup chopped onion
1 teaspoon salt
¼ teaspoon pepper
3 tablespoons oil
11-ounce can tomato-and-mushroom sauce
1-pound can cranberry sauce

Combine beef, matzo meal, water, eggs, onion, salt, and pepper. Form into one-inch meatballs. Using a large skillet, brown meatballs in the oil. Drain off fat. Combine tomato-and-mushroom sauce thoroughly with cranberry sauce. Pour over meatballs and simmer 30 minutes, stirring and basting occasionally. Serve over mashed potatoes. Serves 6 to 8.

SWEET-AND-SOUR MEATBALLS

2 pounds ground beef
⅔ cup matzo meal
½ cup water
2 eggs, slightly beaten
½ cup minced onion
1 teaspoon salt
¼ teaspoon pepper
1 large onion, diced
¼ cup lemon juice
½ cup sugar
11-ounce can tomato-and-mushroom sauce
½ cup water

Combine beef, matzo meal, water, eggs, minced onion, salt, and pepper. Shape into meatballs. In a large pot, combine diced onion, lemon juice, sugar, tomato-and-mushroom sauce, and water. Add meatballs. Bring to a boil, reduce heat, cover, and simmer for about one hour. Serves 6.

YOM TOV MEATBALLS

1 matzo, finely broken
⅓ cup water
1 pound ground beef
1 egg, slightly beaten
1 teaspoon salt
⅛ teaspoon pepper
⅓ cup matzo meal
3 tablespoons vegetable shortening
1 medium onion, diced
¾ cup medium-dry Concord wine
11-ounce can tomato-and mushroom sauce
½ teaspoon sugar

Soak broken matzo in water until water is absorbed. Combine with ground beef, egg, salt, and pepper. Form mixture into about thirty meatballs. Roll them in the matzo meal. Heat shortening in a large skillet. Add meatballs and onion; cook over medium heat until lightly browned on all sides. Combine remaining ingredients; pour over meatballs; cover and simmer 15 minutes. Serves 4.

MEAT CUPS

2 pounds ground beef
2 eggs, slightly beaten
¾ cup matzo meal
1 teaspoon salt
⅛ teaspoon pepper
¼ cup water
2 matzos, finely broken*
3 tablespoons minced onion
3 tablespoons melted chicken fat or pareve margarine
½ teaspoon salt
Dash of pepper
⅓ cup hot water
11-ounce can tomato-and-mushroom sauce

Combine meat with next 5 ingredients. Divide into 6 or 8 portions. Shape into cups and place in a greased baking pan. Mix broken matzos with the next 5 ingredients to make stuffing. Fill meat cups with stuffing. Pour tomato-and-mushroom sauce around the meat cups but not over the stuffing. Bake in a moderate oven (350°F) 45 minutes. Serves 6 to 8.

*1½ cups matzo farfel may be used instead.

HOLISHKES* (STUFFED CABBAGE)

14 to 16 large cabbage leaves
1 pound ground beef
1 matzo, broken**
½ cup water
1 egg, beaten
1 large onion, diced
¼ cup lemon juice
½ cup sugar
¼ cup water
11-ounce can tomato-and-mushroom sauce

Remove leaves from large head of cabbage carefully. Place in a large pot, cover with boiling water, and simmer 5 minutes. Drain. Soak broken matzo in the ½ cup water until soft. Combine this mixture with ground meat and egg. Place a heaping tablespoon of this mixture in the center of each cabbage leaf. Fold in the sides to cover meat; roll. Place cabbage rolls in a large saucepan with open sides down. Combine remaining ingredients and pour over cabbage rolls. Cover; bring to a boil and then reduce heat. Simmer about 1½ hours, basting occasionally. Serves 5 or 6.

*For sugarless Holishkes, omit the sugar and substitute 16 Sucaryl tablets.

**¾ cup matzo farfel may be used instead.

MEATS

STUFFED BEEFBURGERS

1½ 100% whole-wheat matzos
2 tablespoons minced parsley
2 tablespoons minced onion
2 tablespoons chicken fat or pareve margarine
¼ teaspoon salt
¼ cup hot water
1 100% whole-wheat matzo
½ cup cold water
1 pound ground beef
1 egg, slightly beaten
11-ounce can tomato-and-mushroom sauce

Combine first 6 ingredients to make stuffing. Soak remaining matzo in the cold water until soft. Combine this mixture with ground beef and egg. Form meat mixture into 8 patties about 4 inches in diameter. Place stuffing on 4 patties and cover with the other 4. Seal edges. Place in greased baking dish and cover with the tomato-and-mushroom sauce. Bake in a moderate oven (350°F) 45 minutes. Serves 4.

STUFFED PEPPERS

6 medium or 3 large green peppers
1 matzo, broken into small pieces*
¼ cup water
1 pound ground beef
1 egg, slightly beaten
¾ teaspoon salt
⅛ teaspoon pepper
¼ cup minced onion
11-ounce can tomato-and-mushroom sauce
¼ cup water

Wash peppers; remove tops and seeds. If large ones are used, cut in half lengthwise. Soak matzo in the water. Add beef, egg, salt, pepper, onion, and ¼ cup of the tomato-and-mushroom sauce. Fill peppers; place in baking dish with cut side up. Pour balance of sauce over peppers. Add the water to the pan and bake in a moderate oven (375°F) 1¼ hours or until tender, basting occasionally. Serves 6.

*¾ cup matzo farfel may be used instead.

VEAL SAUTERNE

1½ pounds veal cutlet, sliced ¼-inch thick
1½ cups matzo meal
2 eggs beaten with 2 tablespoons cold water
Vegetable shortening or pareve margarine
½ medium green pepper, sliced thin
1 large onion, sliced thin
10½-ounce can condensed clear chicken soup, undiluted
¾ cup sauterne wine

Dip slices of veal first in matzo meal, then in egg mixture, and again in matzo meal. Brown in hot fat in a large skillet. Drain on absorbent paper. After all the veal is browned, wipe excess fat out of skillet. Place veal, green pepper, onion, soup, and wine in the skillet. Cover and simmer 30 minutes or until veal and vegetables are tender. Baste occasionally. Serves 4 to 6.

VEAL WITH PEPPERS

1½ pounds thin-sliced veal cutlet, cut into strips ½-inch wide
½ cup matzo meal
2 small or 1 large green pepper
¼ cup vegetable shortening or pareve margarine
2 large onions, sliced
½ cup sliced mushrooms
½ teaspoon salt
Dash pepper
¼ teaspoon garlic powder
11-ounce can tomato-and-mushroom sauce
¾ cup water

Roll veal strips in matzo meal. Cut green pepper into strips. Heat fat in a large skillet; sauté meat over high heat until browned. Add onions and mushrooms; sprinkle with salt, pepper, and garlic powder. Sauté over low heat 5 minutes. Add tomato-and-mushroom sauce, water, and green pepper. Cover and simmer over low heat 45 minutes or until meat is tender. Serves 4.

VEAL ROLL

½ cup chopped onion
3 tablespoons melted pareve margarine or chicken fat
2 matzos, finely broken*
½ teaspoon salt
⅛ teaspoon pepper
¼ cup minced parsley
¼ cup hot water
3 pounds boned breast of veal
10½-ounce can condensed clear chicken soup, undiluted
Paprika

Mix first 7 ingredients. Spread over veal, leaving a one-half-inch margin on all sides. Roll up and tie with string to hold roll securely. Fasten ends with skewers to hold stuffing. Brown on all sides in hot fat in a Dutch oven. Add undiluted soup to pan. Sprinkle meat generously with paprika. Cover and simmer 2 hours or until tender. Serves 6.

*1½ cups matzo farfel may be used instead.

TOMATO VEAL CUTLETS

2 pounds veal cutlets
11-ounce can tomato-and-mushroom sauce
1 cup matzo meal
½ teaspoon salt
⅛ teaspoon pepper

Mix matzo meal with salt and pepper. Dip cutlets in tomato-and-mushroom sauce; roll in matzo-meal mixture. Chill in refrigerator at least one-half hour. Fry in hot fat in a large skillet, over low heat, until tender and brown. Serves 4 to 6.

STUFFED BREAST OF VEAL

4½- to 5-pound breast of veal
1 large onion, diced
½ cup diced celery
2 tablespoons chicken fat
2 tablespoons minced parsley
1 cup matzo meal
¾ teaspoon salt
Dash white pepper
1¾ cups hot water
1 egg, beaten
11-ounce can tomato-and-mushroom sauce
1 sauce can water
1 teaspoon paprika

Have butcher cut a pocket in the veal. Sauté onion and celery in chicken fat until onion is golden brown. Add parsley, matzo meal, salt, pepper, hot water, and beaten egg. Fill veal pocket with this mixture. Fasten with skewers or sew opening with heavy white thread. Place in a roasting pan. Add the tomato-and-mushroom sauce plus water. Sprinkle meat with the paprika. Cover pan. Place in a moderate oven (350°F) and roast about 2½ hours or until tender, basting occasionally. Uncover during last half-hour to brown meat. Serves 6 to 8.

VEAL NUGGETS WITH SAUCE PIQUANT

2 pounds ground veal
½ cup matzo meal
1 egg, slightly beaten
2 egg whites (save yolks for sauce)
¼ cup water
2 tablespoons minced parsley
1 teaspoon salt
¼ teaspoon pepper
⅓ cup matzo meal
3 tablespoons peanut oil
3 tablespoons pareve margarine

Combine veal with the ½ cup matzo meal, egg, egg whites, water, parsley, salt, and pepper. Shape in 1½-inch balls. Roll in the remaining matzo meal. Heat oil and margarine in a large skillet. Brown veal nuggets on all sides; reduce heat and cook 15 minutes longer, shaking pan frequently. Serve with Sauce Piquant. Serves 4 to 6.

SAUCE PIQUANT

2 tablespoons potato starch
⅔ cup water
10½-ounce can condensed clear chicken soup
2 egg yolks
3 tablespoons lemon juice

Combine potato starch with a small amount of the water. Bring the balance of the water and soup to a boil; reduce heat. Add starch mixture to soup very gradually, stirring constantly. Heat and stir until thickened. Remove from heat. Beat egg yolks and lemon juice together. Add a little of the hot mixture and stir rapidly. Then combine with the hot mixture, stirring constantly. Over very low heat, stir and cook until thickened again. DO NOT BOIL. Serve with Veal Nuggets. Serves 4 to 6.

BREADED VEAL CUTLET

1½ pounds veal cutlet, sliced ¼-inch thick
1½ cups matzo meal
2 eggs, beaten with 2 tablespoons cold water
Chicken fat, vegetable shortening, or peanut oil

Dip slices of veal first in matzo meal, then in egg mixture, and again in matzo meal. Place in refrigerator for at least one-half hour. Fry slowly in hot fat in a large skillet until tender and golden brown. Serves 4 to 6.

VEAL ROLLS SAUTERNE

2 pounds ground veal
½ cup matzo meal
2 eggs, slightly beaten
¼ cup water
¼ cup minced parsley
1 teaspoon salt
½ teaspoon ginger
Matzo meal
10½-ounce can condensed clear chicken soup, undiluted
¾ cup sauterne

Combine veal, ½ cup matzo meal, eggs, water, minced parsley, salt, and ginger. Shape into 12 rolls, about 3 inches long. Roll in matzo meal. Brown in a small amount of fat. Blend soup and wine; pour over meat. Cover and bring to a boil and simmer about 30 minutes. Serves 6.

CREOLE VEAL CUTLETS OR LAMB CHOPS

6 large veal cutlets (2½ pounds) or 6 large shoulder lamb chops (3 pounds)
½ cup matzo meal
11-ounce can tomato-and-mushroom sauce
½ cup minced onion
½ cup finely chopped celery
½ cup finely chopped green pepper

Coat meat with matzo meal. Brown in a small amount of hot fat. Place in a covered baking dish. Combine tomato-and-mushroom sauce, onion, celery, and green pepper. Spoon over meat. Cover and bake in a moderate oven (350°F) for one hour or until tender. Serves 6.

STUFFED BREAST OF LAMB

4 to 5 pounds breast of lamb
1 large onion, minced
½ cup minced celery
2 tablespoons chicken fat
2 tablespoons minced parsley
1 cup matzo meal
1 teaspoon salt
Dash pepper
1½ cups hot water
1 egg, beaten
11-ounce can tomato-and-mushroom sauce
1 sauce can water
Paprika, garlic powder, and salt

Have butcher cut a pocket in each breast of lamb. Sauté onion and celery in chicken fat until onion is golden brown. Add parsley, matzo meal, salt, pepper, hot water, and egg. Fill lamb pockets with this mixture. Fasten with skewers or sew openings with heavy white thread. Place in roasting pan. Add tomato-and-mushroom sauce plus water. Sprinkle with paprika, garlic powder, and salt. Place in a moderate oven (350°F), cover, and roast about 2½ hours or until tender, basting occasionally. Uncover during last 45 minutes to brown meat. Skim excess fat from gravy before serving. Serves 6 to 8.

4 large lamb shanks
¼ cup matzo meal or cake meal
½ teaspoon salt
Dash pepper
¼ teaspoon garlic powder
2 tablespoons vegetable shortening
1-pound jar stewed prunes, pitted
¾ cup juice from prunes
¼ cup sugar
3 tablespoons cider vinegar
1 teaspoon cinnamon
¼ teaspoon ginger
½ teaspoon salt

SPICED LAMB SHANKS

Roll shanks in mixture of meal, salt, pepper, and garlic powder. Brown in shortening. Place in roasting pan with prune juice. Cover tightly and bake at 325°F about 1½ hours or until meat is almost tender, basting occasionally. Mix prunes, sugar, vinegar, cinnamon, ginger, and salt. Skim fat away from gravy. Add fruit. Cover and bake 30 minutes, basting occasionally. Serves 4.

SHISH KEBABS

2 pounds boneless shoulder lamb, cut into 1¼-inch cubes
½ cup medium-dry Concord wine
¼ teaspoon pepper
1 large onion, finely minced
¼ cup peanut oil
2 tablespoons cider vinegar
Firm tomatoes cut into thick wedges
Small white onions, parboiled
Whole mushroom caps
Green pepper, cut into 1¼-inch squares

Mix wine, pepper, minced onion, peanut oil, and vinegar. Pour over lamb cubes. Cover and place in refrigerator for at least three hours or overnight. Using 10- or 12-inch skewers, arrange meat and vegetables alternately. Broil slowly until meat and vegetables are tender, turning when necessary. Baste occasionally with the leftover wine mixture. Serve on Savory Matzo Farfel (page 144). Serves 5 or 6.

---

1 cup minced onion
½ cup diced celery
6 tablespoons pareve margarine
6 matzos, finely broken*
½ teaspoon salt
⅛ teaspoon pepper
2 teaspoons paprika
1 egg, slightly beaten
1 can condensed clear chicken soup, undiluted
1-pound jar stewed prunes (20), drained, pitted, and chopped
6 large shoulder lamb chops, koshered

LAMB CHOPS ON PRUNE STUFFING

Sauté onion and celery in margarine until tender. Add broken matzos and toast lightly. Combine salt, pepper, paprika, eggs, and soup. Add to matzos. Fold in chopped prunes. Spread in a greased shallow baking pan. Brown chops in a hot skillet. Arrange chops on stuffing and cover pan, using aluminum foil if pan has no cover. Bake in a moderate oven (325°F) one hour or until chops are tender. Serves 6.

*4 cups matzo farfel may be used instead.

LAMB CHOPS À L'ORANGE

6 large shoulder lamb chops, cut 1-inch thick, koshered
¼ cup matzo meal
Salt and pepper
2 tablespoons peanut oil or vegetable shortening
¼ teaspoon ginger
1 cup orange juice
1 tablespoon grated orange rind
2 tablespoons sugar
2 oranges, peeled and sectioned

Coat lamb chops with matzo meal. Sprinkle with salt and pepper if desired. Brown in hot fat in a large skillet. Add mixture of ginger, orange juice, orange rind, and sugar. Cover and bake at 350°F about 45 minutes or until tender, basting occasionally. Add orange sections and heat a few minutes. Serves 6.

FESTIVE BRAISED LAMB CHOPS

4 medium potatoes, peeled
4 large shoulder lamb chops, 1-inch thick, koshered
¼ cup chopped onion
1 tablespoon chicken fat or pareve margarine
¼ teaspoon pepper
½ cup sauterne wine
½ cup canned tomato-and-mushroom sauce
½ cup canned clear chicken soup, undiluted

Boil potatoes in salted water until almost tender. Cool and slice. In a large skillet, cook onion in the fat until tender. Place onions in a 9×12-inch baking pan. In the same skillet, brown chops on all sides, adding a little fat if necessary. Place in baking dish. Mix pepper, wine, tomato-and-mushroom sauce, and soup. Pour over chops. Arrange potato slices on top and around chops. Bake in a moderate oven (350°F) for 45 minutes or until tender and potatoes are lightly browned. Serve with the pan gravy. Serves 4.

BRAISED LAMB SHANKS

4 large lamb shanks
¼ cup matzo meal or cake meal
¼ teaspoon salt
Dash pepper
¼ teaspoon garlic powder
2 tablespoons vegetable shortening
½ cup diced onion
11-ounce can tomato-and-mushroom sauce

Roll shanks in mixture of meal, salt, pepper, and garlic powder. In a roasting pan, melt fat. Brown shanks. Pour off fat. Add onion plus tomato-and-mushroom sauce. Cover tightly and simmer on top of stove or bake in a slow oven (300°F) 1½ hours or until tender, basting occasionally. Serves 4.

LAMB CHOPS AND POTATO BAKE

4 thick round-bone lamb chops
¼ cup matzo meal or cake meal
1 cup prune juice
1 tablespoon lemon juice
½ teaspoon salt
¼ teaspoon pepper
¼ teaspoon cinnamon
¼ teaspoon ginger
1 medium onion, sliced thin
4 medium potatoes, peeled and quartered

Coat chops with the meal. In a large skillet, brown chops in a small amount of hot fat. Drain off excess fat. Combine prune juice, lemon juice, salt, pepper, cinnamon, and ginger; pour over meat. Add onions and potatoes. Cover and simmer one hour, basting potatoes occasionally. Serves 4.

ALMOND-RAISIN SAUCE FOR TONGUE

½ cup white raisins
10½-ounce can condensed clear chicken soup, undiluted
¼ cup sugar
1 tablespoon pareve margarine
1½ tablespoons grated orange rind
1 tablespoon potato starch mixed with ½ cup water
¾ cup blanched, slivered almonds

Cook raisins in chicken soup until plumped. Add sugar, margarine, orange rind, and potato-starch mixture. Stir over low heat about one minute or until thickened. Blend in almonds; heat. Serve hot on sliced tongue. Serves 6.

APRICOT-RAISIN SAUCE FOR TONGUE

This is a modern version of an original recipe that involved long cooking and pureeing. This tastes every bit as marvelous and takes almost no work or time at all.

1 large onion, finely diced
¾ cup white raisins
12-ounce jar apricot preserves
1 tablespoon lemon juice
Pinch salt

Combine all ingredients and cook over low heat until raisins are plumped and mixture is thick. Serve hot on sliced tongue. Serves 6.

SWEET-AND-SOUR LAMB TONGUES

12 lamb tongues
¼ cup cider vinegar
1 large onion, diced
¼ cup lemon juice
½ cup sugar
11-ounce can tomato-and-mushroom sauce
½ cup water

Place tongues in a large saucepan; cover with cold water and add vinegar. Bring to a boil and then simmer for about one-half hour or until skin can be easily removed from tongues. Run cold water over tongues until they are cool enough to handle. Remove skin and trim excess fat. Return to saucepan; add onion, lemon juice, sugar, tomato-and-mushroom sauce, and water. Cover and simmer about one hour or until tender. Serves 4 to 6.

LIVER CUTLETS

1½ pounds liver
2 eggs, slightly beaten
½ cup diced onion
½ cup matzo meal
1 teaspoon salt
⅛ teaspoon pepper
¼ cup chicken fat or pareve margarine

Broil liver, remove skin; grind. Combine with eggs, onion, matzo meal, salt, and pepper. Shape into 8 patties. Coat with additional matzo meal. Fry in the hot fat until browned on both sides. Serve with Onion Sauce. Serves 4.

ONION SAUCE

2 large onions, sliced
¼ cup chicken fat
2 tablespoons potato starch
10½-ounce can condensed clear chicken soup, undiluted
½ cup water
Salt and pepper

Cook onion in fat until tender but not brown. Mix potato starch with a few tablespoons of the cold chicken soup. Add this mixture, plus the balance of the chicken soup and the water, to the onions. Cook over moderate heat, stirring constantly, until sauce thickens. Season to taste. Serve on Liver Cutlets. Also good with leftover turkey, chicken, or veal.

BRAISED LIVER

1½ pounds liver, sliced
¼ cup matzo meal or cake meal
3 tablespoons chicken fat or vegetable shortening
2 large onions, sliced
1 teaspoon salt
⅛ teaspoon pepper
4 medium potatoes, peeled and quartered
2 cups tomato juice

Broil liver and remove skin. Cut into 1½-inch strips. Roll in meal. Brown onions in fat. Add liver and brown. Add salt, pepper, potatoes, and tomato juice. Cover and cook about 45 minutes or until potatoes and liver are tender. Stir frequently. Serves 4.

FESTIVE LIVER RING

1½ pounds liver
2 medium onions
¾ cup matzo meal
2 eggs, slightly beaten
¾ teaspoon salt
⅛ teaspoon pepper
10½-ounce can condensed clear chicken soup, undiluted
11-ounce can tomato-and-mushroom sauce

Broil liver and remove skin. Put through meat grinder with the onions. Add matzo meal, eggs, salt, pepper, chicken soup, and ¼ cup of the tomato-and-mushroom sauce. Pack into a well-greased 6-cup ring mold. (For extra ease in removal, mold may be lined with oiled cheesecloth.) Bake in a moderate oven (350°F) 45 minutes. Turn out on a platter; fill center with cooked and seasoned carrot slices. Serve with the balance of the tomato-and-mushroom sauce, heated. Serves 6.

STUFFED MILTZ

1 miltz
1 large onion, diced
2 tablespoons chicken fat or pareve margarine
1 cup matzo meal
1 teaspoon salt
Dash pepper
1½ cups hot water
1 egg, beaten
Salt, pepper, paprika, garlic powder
2 medium onions, sliced
2 tablespoons chicken fat or pareve margarine

Have butcher cut pocket in miltz. Sauté diced onion in two tablespoons of chicken fat until tender. Mix with matzo meal, salt, pepper, hot water, and egg. Fill miltz lightly, allowing room for stuffing to expand. Sew up opening. Sprinkle with salt, pepper, paprika, and garlic powder. Place in a roasting pan with sliced onion and fat. Add 1 cup boiling water. Prick all over with a fork. Bake at 350°F for 2 hours or until firm and a brown crust forms, basting occasionally. Serves 5 or 6.

FRANKFURTER-SWEET POTATO-APPLE CASSEROLE

6 medium (3 pounds) sweet potatoes
2 cups applesauce
¾ teaspoon cinnamon
¼ cup sugar
1 pound frankfurters, sliced
2 tablespoons chicken fat or pareve margarine

Cook, peel, and slice potatoes. Mix applesauce, cinnamon, and sugar. In a greased 2-quart baking dish, arrange alternate layers of sweet potato, applesauce, and sliced frankfurters, beginning and ending with sweet potato. Dot the top with the chicken fat or margarine. Bake in a moderate oven (375°F) 30 minutes or until bubbling. Serves 4 to 6.

POULTRY

POULTRY

For many second-generation Jewish people, chicken has a negative connotation. Every Shabbat, every Yom Tov, every wedding, and every Bar Mitzvah at one time meant "roast" chicken, which was not really roast chicken at all, and which always tasted the same—like straw. First the quartered chicken was boiled nearly to death to make soup; then it was put in a roasting pan with vegetables and liquid, seasoned, and potted in the oven until brown. Any resemblance to real roast chicken was purely imaginary.

Poultry can become a family favorite if you prepare it well. Use the chicken from the soup pot in a salad, casserole, blintz, or other recipe that calls for cooked diced poultry. If you relish boiled chicken, enjoy it in good health. Just don't try to "roast" it afterward, please.

To be fair, remember that years ago women made chicken this way because they could not afford to buy extra for the soup. Even when their daughters were able to spend the money, they continued to cook as they had learned at home. But you do not have to continue the custom.

POT-ROASTED STUFFED CHICKEN

4½- to 5-pound roasting chicken
1 medium onion, diced
½ cup diced celery
1½ tablespoons chicken fat or pareve margarine
1¼ cups matzo meal
2 tablespoons chopped parsley
½ teaspoon salt
Dash pepper
1 egg, slightly beaten
10½-ounce can condensed clear chicken soup, undiluted
4 potatoes, peeled and parboiled
4 carrots, sliced and parboiled
8 small white onions, parboiled
1 teaspoon paprika
¼ teaspoon garlic
½ teaspoon salt
⅛ teaspoon pepper

Sauté onion and celery in chicken fat until tender. Combine with matzo meal, parsley, salt, and pepper. Mix half of the can of soup with the egg; add to matzo-meal mixture. Stuff chicken loosely and truss. Brown on all sides in a small amount of chicken fat or pareve margarine in a heavy kettle or Dutch oven. Pour off fat. Add the remaining half can of soup. Cover and simmer one hour, breast-side-up. Add vegetables and the remaining 4 seasonings. Simmer about one hour longer or until tender. Add water if necessary. Serves 4 to 6.

BAKED CHICKEN WITH MUSHROOMS

3-pound frying chicken
3 tablespoons chicken fat or pareve margarine
½ teaspoon onion powder
⅛ teaspoon garlic powder
10½-ounce can condensed clear chicken soup, undiluted
¼ pound mushrooms, diced
3 tablespoons water
2 tablespoons potato starch

Cut chicken into quarters. Heat the fat in a large skillet. Add chicken and sauté until brown. Place chicken in a baking dish. To the fat in the skillet, add onion powder, garlic powder, and condensed soup. Blend water with potato starch until smooth. Gradually add this mixture to soup mixture and cook, stirring constantly, until thickened. Add mushrooms and gravy to chicken. Cover (use aluminum foil if pan has no cover) and bake in a moderate oven (350°F) one hour or until tender. Serves 3 or 4.

CHICKEN CACCIATORE

1 large frying chicken, cut up
½ cup matzo meal
1 teaspoon salt
¼ teaspoon pepper
¼ cup peanut oil
1 cup sliced onion
1 medium green pepper, chopped
½ teaspoon garlic powder
½ pound mushrooms, sliced
1 pound cooked or canned peeled tomatoes
½ cup canned condensed clear chicken soup, undiluted

Mix matzo meal with salt and pepper. Dip chicken parts in water and then roll in meal mixture. Heat oil in a large skillet and brown chicken parts three or four at a time. Place all the chicken in the skillet. Add onion, green pepper, garlic powder, mushrooms, tomatoes, and chicken soup. Cover and cook 30 to 40 minutes or until tender. Serves 3 or 4.

CHICKEN PAPRIKA WITH FLUFFY POTATO KNAIDLACH

4-pound roasting chicken, cut up
½ cup matzo meal or cake meal
1 teaspoon salt
¼ teaspoon pepper
¼ cup peanut oil
3 large onions, sliced
10½-ounce can condensed clear chicken soup, undiluted
2 tablespoons paprika
¼ teaspoon garlic powder
6 young carrots, sliced

Roll chicken parts in a mixture of the meal, salt, and pepper. Brown a few pieces at a time in the hot oil in a large pot or Dutch oven. Remove pieces as they brown. When all chicken is browned, sauté onion until tender. If oil is too dark, discard and use 2 tablespoons fresh oil to sauté onion. Stir in soup, paprika, and garlic powder; bring to a boil. Add chicken and carrots. Cover and simmer 45 minutes or until chicken is tender. Serve with Fluffy Potato Knaidlach (page 50). Serves 4 to 6.

EPICUREAN CHICKEN

1 large frying chicken, cut up
¼ cup cake meal or matzo meal
½ teaspoon salt
⅛ teaspoon pepper
¼ cup chicken fat or pareve margarine
6 scallions, sliced
¼ pound mushrooms, sliced
2 tablespoons lemon juice
1 teaspoon sugar
½ cup apple juice
2 medium tomatoes, peeled and diced

Roll chicken parts in a mixture of the meal, salt, and pepper. Heat the fat in a large skillet. Brown chicken in the hot fat and remove pieces as they are done. Pour off all but about 1½ tablespoons of the fat. Sauté the scallions and mushrooms for a few minutes. Combine lemon juice, sugar, and apple juice. Add chicken, lemon-juice mixture, and tomatoes to the skillet. Cover and simmer over low heat about one hour or until tender. Serves 3 or 4.

BAKED BROILERS WITH MATZO-NUT STUFFING

1 cup minced onion
½ cup diced celery
½ cup coarsely chopped nuts
6 tablespoons pareve margarine or chicken fat
5 matzos, finely broken*
½ teaspoon salt
⅛ teaspoon pepper
2 teaspoons paprika
1 egg, slightly beaten
1 cup canned condensed clear chicken soup, undiluted
2 broilers, split in half

Sauté onion, celery, and nuts in the fat until the onion is tender but not browned. Add broken matzos and toast lightly. Combine seasonings, egg, and condensed soup. Add to matzo mixture. Spread in a large greased baking dish or roasting pan. Place broiler halves on top. Brush with melted fat and sprinkle with salt and pepper. Bake in a moderate oven (350°F) 1 to 1½ hours or until tender and golden brown. Serves 4 to 6.

*3¾ cups matzo farfel may be used instead.

GAN EDEN CHICKEN

2 large frying chickens, cut up
1 cup matzo meal
1 teaspoon salt
¼ teaspoon pepper
½ cup peanut oil
2 cups chopped onion
4 cups applesauce
1 cup orange juice
2 teaspoons grated orange rind
1 teaspoon cinnamon
1 cup blanched, slivered almonds

Roll chicken parts in a mixture of the matzo meal, salt, and pepper. Fry in the hot oil, in a large skillet, until brown on all sides. Remove chicken from pan as pieces are browned. When all chicken is browned, drain off all but about 2 tablespoons of the fat. Add onions and cook until tender. Return chicken to pan. Mix applesauce, orange juice, orange rind, and cinnamon. Pour over chicken; cover and cook about 30 minutes or until tender. Add almonds and cook 5 minutes. Serves 6 to 8.

SMOTHERED CHICKEN

4- to 5-pound pullet, cut up
½ cup matzo meal
½ teaspoon salt
⅛ teaspoon pepper
¼ teaspoon garlic powder
¼ cup peanut oil
1 large onion, sliced
3 stalks celery, chopped
1 large carrot, diced
1 cup mushrooms, sliced
10½-ounce can condensed clear chicken soup, undiluted

Roll chicken in a mixture of the matzo meal, salt, pepper, and garlic powder. Brown in hot peanut oil in a large skillet. Place chicken in small roasting pan or Dutch oven. In the same skillet, in the remaining oil, sauté the onion, celery, carrot, and mushrooms until onion is tender. Place in pan with chicken; heat chicken soup and add. Cover and bake at 325°F for 1½ hours or until tender. Serves 4 to 6.

LEMON BAKED CHICKEN

1 frying chicken, cut up
1 whole lemon
¾ cup matzo meal
1½ teaspoons salt
¾ teaspoon paprika
1 egg
2 tablespoons water
Peanut oil or vegetable shortening
2 tablespoons sugar
1 unpeeled lemon, sliced thin
10½-ounce can condensed clear chicken soup, undiluted

Grate rind of the whole lemon. Set aside. Cut lemon in half and squeeze juice of both halves over chicken. Mix matzo meal with salt and paprika. Beat egg with water. Dip chicken first in egg mixture and then in meal mixture. Brown slowly in a large skillet in one-fourth inch of hot oil or vegetable shortening. Place in a small roasting pan or large covered casserole. Sprinkle the grated lemon rind over the chicken, making sure to put some on each piece. Sprinkle with sugar and arrange sliced lemon on chicken. Add condensed clear chicken soup. Cover and bake in a moderate oven (375°F) about 30 minutes or until chicken is tender. Serves 3 or 4.

BROILED CHICKEN

1 broiler, split in half
¼ teaspoon black pepper
2 tablespoons melted pareve margarine or chicken fat

Sprinkle chicken halves with the pepper. Place on broiler pan, skin-side-down. Brush with some of the melted fat. Place pan about six inches from the heat. Broil about 20 minutes. Turn; brush skin with remaining fat; broil 20 minutes longer or until bird is well browned and flesh is tender. If bird browns too fast, reduce heat or move farther from the heat.

HONEYED CHICKEN

½ cup peanut oil
2 eggs
2 tablespoons water
2 fryers, cut up
1 cup matzo meal
1 teaspoon salt
⅛ teaspoon pepper
1 cup hot water
¼ cup honey
1 cup orange juice

Heat oil in skillet or frying pan. Beat eggs and the 2 tablespoons water together. Mix matzo meal, salt, and pepper. Dip chicken in egg mixture and then roll in matzo-meal mixture. Brown in hot oil. Remove to a Dutch oven or covered roaster. Mix hot water, honey, and orange juice. Pour over chicken and cover. Simmer slowly on top of stove or place in a moderate oven (325°F) about 45 minutes or until tender. Baste occasionally. Serves 6 to 8.

GLAZED CHICKEN WITH MATZO-NUT STUFFING

1 large roasting chicken
⅓ cup pareve margarine or chicken fat
⅓ cup minced onion
⅓ cup finely chopped celery
⅓ cup chopped almonds
4 matzos, broken*
½ teaspoon salt
⅛ teaspoon pepper
1 egg
10½-ounce can condensed clear chicken soup, undiluted
1 tablespoon grated orange rind

GLAZE

1 cup orange juice
2 teaspoons grated orange rind
¼ cup honey
¼ cup chicken fat or pareve margarine

Sauté onion, celery, and nuts in the ⅓ cup of fat until vegetables are tender. Add broken matzos and toast lightly. Combine salt, pepper, egg, chicken soup, and orange rind in a large bowl. Add matzo mixture and mix well. Use to fill the chicken. Place filled bird on a rack in an open roasting pan with breast side down for first half of roasting time. Combine ingredients for glaze and pour over chicken. Roast in a slow oven (325°F) about 2½ hours or until browned and tender. Baste frequently. Serves 4 to 6.

*2½ cups matzo farfel may be used instead.

FRIED CHICKEN

1 large frying chicken, cut up
¾ cup matzo meal
¾ teaspoon salt
¼ teaspoon pepper
1 teaspoon paprika
1 egg
2 tablespoons water
Peanut oil or vegetable shortening

Combine matzo meal, salt, pepper, and paprika. Beat egg and and water together. Dip chicken parts in egg mixture and then in matzo-meal mixture, coating completely. Place chicken in refrigerator for at least one-half hour, as this helps coating to adhere well. Heat one-half inch of oil or shortening in a large skillet. Brown chicken parts, starting with meaty pieces first. (This takes about 20 minutes.) Then cover tightly and continue to cook over low heat until tender, about 20 to 30 minutes longer. Or, if preferred, after browning, place in a 350°F oven in a large, shallow, uncovered pan for about 30 minutes or until tender. Brush with additional fat occasionally. Serves 3 or 4.

OVEN-FRIED CHICKEN

1 fryer, cut up
1 cup matzo meal
1 teaspoon salt
¼ teaspoon pepper
1½ teaspoons paprika
⅓ cup chicken fat or pareve margarine

Combine matzo meal with salt, pepper, and paprika. Dip each piece of chicken in melted fat and then in meal mixture. Place chicken, skin-side-up, in a well-greased, large, shallow, uncovered baking pan without overlapping pieces. Bake in a moderate oven (350°F) about one hour or until golden brown and tender. For crisp crust, slip pan under broiler for a few minutes before serving. Serves 3 or 4.

FARFEL CHICKEN CASSEROLE

3 tablespoons chicken fat or pareve margarine
1 large onion, diced
10½-ounce can condensed clear chicken soup, undiluted
1 cup liquid from the cooked vegetables (see below)
½ teaspoon salt
Dash white pepper
2 to 3 cups diced, cooked chicken (or turkey)
2 cups cooked, sliced carrots
1 cup cooked, diced celery
1¼ cups matzo farfel

Sauté onion in the fat until tender. Add soup, vegetable liquid, and seasonings. Arrange chicken, vegetables, matzo farfel, and sauce in alternate layers in a 2-quart casserole. Cover and bake in a hot oven (425°F) 30 minutes. Serves 6 to 8.

CHICKEN CUTLETS WITH TOMATO-AND-MUSHROOM SAUCE

2 matzos, broken into small pieces
10½-ounce can condensed clear chicken soup, undiluted
2½ cups ground chicken (or turkey)
2 eggs, beaten
2 tablespoons minced parsley
1 cup matzo meal
Pareve margarine or chicken fat
11-ounce can tomato-and-mushroom sauce

Soak broken matzos in condensed soup until liquid is absorbed. Combine with chicken, eggs, and parsley. Shape into 8 cutlets. Coat each cutlet with matzo meal by holding it in your hand and sprinkling the matzo meal on all sides. Sauté in pareve margarine or chicken fat until golden brown on both sides. Serve with heated tomato-and-mushroom sauce. Serves 4.

CHICKEN À LA DEBORAH

¼ cup minced onion
1 cup diced celery
2 tablespoons chicken fat
3 cups diced, cooked chicken
1 tablespoon potato starch
1 tablespoon cold water
10½-ounce can condensed clear chicken soup, undiluted
1 recipe Puff Shells (page 170)

Sauté onion and celery in chicken fat until onion is tender but not browned. Add diced chicken. Combine potato starch and cold water. Gradually stir in condensed chicken soup. Add soup mixture to chicken mixture. Stir occasionally and cook over low heat until sauce is thickened. Fill cooled Puff Shells (page 170) and replace tops. Serves 6 or 7.

CHICKEN À LA PRINCESS ON POTATO LATKES

3 tablespoons chicken fat or pareve margarine
½ cup diced green pepper
½ cup chopped onion
1 cup sliced mushrooms
3 cups diced cooked chicken (or turkey)
1 tablespoon potato starch
1 tablespoon cold water
10½-ounce can condensed clear chicken soup, undiluted
6-ounce (or two 3-ounce) package potato-pancake mix
2¼ cups water
2 eggs

Sauté green pepper, onion, and mushrooms in the fat until tender but not browned. Add diced chicken (or turkey). Combine potato starch with the water; gradually stir in the chicken soup. Add this mixture to chicken mixture. Stir and cook over low heat until sauce is thickened. Season to taste. Make potato pancakes as directed on package. Top them with Chicken à la Princess. Serves 6.

HOT CHICKEN LOAF

10½-ounce can condensed clear chicken soup, undiluted
1 soup can water
2½ cups matzo farfel
1 medium onion, diced
2 tablespoons diced green pepper
2 tablespoons chicken fat
3 to 4 cups ground, cooked chicken
1 teaspoon salt
1 teaspoon paprika
3 eggs, beaten
11-ounce can tomato-and-mushroom sauce

Combine chicken soup and water; add matzo farfel and set aside for at least 10 minutes. Sauté onion and green pepper in chicken fat until tender. Combine all ingredients except the tomato-and-mushroom sauce. Grease a loaf pan or 8-inch-square pan thoroughly and line it on the bottom. Pack the chicken mixture into the pan, leaving about one-half inch head room. Bake in a moderate oven (350°F) one hour. Remove from oven and let loaf remain in pan for 10 minutes. Loosen sides with spatula. Turn loaf out on a platter. Serve with heated tomato-and-mushroom sauce. Serves 6 to 8.

STUFFED ROCK CORNISH HENS

The amount of fat in this recipe looks excessive, but remember, Rock Cornish Hens have little or no fat of their own. They will be dry unless it is supplemented.

6 Rock Cornish hens (1 pound each)
½ cup chicken fat or pareve margarine
½ cup diced onion
1 cup diced mushrooms
6 matzos, finely broken
¾ teaspoon salt
⅛ teaspoon pepper
1 tablespoon paprika
1 egg, slightly beaten
10½-ounce can condensed clear chicken soup, undiluted
Chicken fat or pareve margarine

Sauté onion and mushrooms in the fat until tender but not browned. Add broken matzos and toast lightly. Combine salt, pepper, paprika, egg, and soup. Add to matzo mixture. Lightly fill body cavities with stuffing. Close openings with skewers. Place on a rack in a large roasting pan, breast-side-up. Brush liberally with chicken fat or pareve margarine. Roast uncovered in a hot oven (425°F), brushing occasionally with additional fat, for one hour or until tender. Serves 6.

ORANGE BRAISED DUCK

The browning of the ducks takes a long time, so don't get impatient. This is the main secret to moist duck which is not greasy. Most of the thick fat layer under the skin can be extracted in this way.

2 large ducks, quartered
2 teaspoons salt
¼ teaspoon pepper
2 cups orange juice
10½-ounce can condensed clear chicken soup, undiluted
½ cup water
1 cup (12-ounce jar) orange marmalade
¼ cup potato starch
¼ cup cold water

Brown duck in a roasting pan, without adding fat. Pour off fat as it cooks out. To the duck, add salt, pepper, orange juice, chicken soup, and the ½ cup water. Cover and bake in a slow oven (325°F) for 1½ hours or until tender. Remove duck from roaster and keep warm in the oven. Skim all fat from gravy. Add marmalade to gravy and stir until dissolved. Add potato starch mixed with the ¼ cup cold water. Cook until smooth and thickened. Pour sauce over duck and serve. Serves 4 to 8.

HONEYED DUCK WITH ORANGE SAUCE

2 large ducks
½ cup honey
2 teaspoons paprika

Sprinkle ducks with salt and pepper. Place on a rack in an uncovered roasting pan and place in a moderate oven (350°F) for 2½ hours, turning to brown evenly. Drain off fat from pan. Mix honey with paprika. Brush ducks on all sides with half of this mixture. Turn ducks after 15 minutes and brush with remaining honey mixture. Bake until skin is crisp and brown, about 15 minutes longer. Serve with Orange Sauce. Serves 4 to 8.

ORANGE SAUCE FOR HONEYED DUCK

Giblets and necks from 2 ducks
¾ cup canned condensed clear chicken soup, undiluted
¾ cup water
2 tablespoons potato starch
¾ cup orange juice
¼ cup honey
½ teaspoon salt
2 teaspoons grated orange rind
Dash ginger

Cook giblets and necks in the chicken soup and water until tender. Mix potato starch with a little of the orange juice. Then mix with balance of orange juice. Add ¾ cup of the giblet broth, the honey, salt, orange rind, and ginger. Cook over low heat, stirring constantly, until thickened. Serve hot with duck. Serves 6.

BASIC MATZO STUFFING

¾ cup vegetable shortening, chicken fat, or pareve margarine
¾ cup minced onion
10 matzos, finely broken*
1 teaspoon salt
¼ teaspoon pepper
1 tablespoon paprika
1 egg
1½ cans (2 cups) condensed clear chicken soup, undiluted**

Sauté onion in fat until tender but not browned. Add broken matzos and toast lightly. Combine seasonings, egg, and soup. Add to matzo mixture. Enough for a 10- to 12-pound bird.

*7 cups matzo farfel may be used instead.

**This makes a dry dressing. If you prefer a moist stuffing, increase the condensed chicken soup to 2 cans.

VARIATIONS

CELERY STUFFING: Sauté 1 cup diced celery with the onion.

MUSHROOM STUFFING: Sauté 1 cup diced fresh mushrooms with the onion.

NUT STUFFING: Toast 1½ cups coarsely chopped nuts with the onion before adding matzo crumbs.

GIBLET STUFFING: Cook giblets in water until tender. Mince and add to dressing.

FRUIT STUFFING: Add 1-pound jar stewed prunes, drained, pitted, and chopped, plus 2 cups pared, diced apple and ½ cup raisins.

---

1 cup diced celery
1 cup diced onion
¼ cup chicken fat or pareve margarine
3 cups matzo farfel*
½ cup canned condensed clear chicken soup, heated
1 teaspoon salt
1 egg, slightly beaten
1-pound can cranberry sauce

CRANBERRY STUFFING

Sauté celery and onion in fat until lightly browned. Add farfel and toast lightly. Combine hot chicken soup with salt and add to farfel mixture. Break up cranberry sauce with a fork and combine with the egg. Add to farfel mixture.

Makes enough for a large capon or two small ducks. For a turkey, double the recipe.

*4 matzos, broken, may be used instead.

---

1 large onion, diced
¾ cup diced celery
3 tablespoons chicken fat
2½ cups matzo meal
¼ cup chopped parsley
1 teaspoon salt
⅛ teaspoon pepper
2 eggs, slightly beaten
10½-ounce can condensed clear chicken soup, undiluted

PARSLEY STUFFING

Sauté onion and celery in the chicken fat until tender. Remove from heat. Add matzo meal, parsley, and seasonings. Combine beaten eggs and the condensed soup and add to the matzo-meal mixture. Fill bird loosely; do not pack.

Makes enough for a large capon. For a large chicken, use about half the recipe.

"OTHER MEALS" MAIN DISHES

"OTHER MEALS" MAIN DISHES

Dinner is dinner, but the other meals for Passover have always presented women with their most exasperating challenge. How many times can you serve latkes, salami and eggs, or reheated leftovers from last night's meal? It does not have to be that way. With a little of this and some of that and a lot of imagination, other meals can be as exciting as the more elaborate, more expensive dinners.

Besides the recipes given in this chapter, blintzes and latkes are perfect for light meals. Take a look at the recipes in the Fried Things chapter (page 106) and some of the salads in the Salads, Dressings, and Relishes chapter (page 118) for additional ideas.

"OTHER MEALS" MAIN DISHES

CREAMY MARMALADE OMELET

For a creamy, puffy omelet every time, try this recipe. Use different fillings if you wish, but be sure to make this one.

6 large eggs
½ cup sour cream
½ teaspoon salt
2 tablespoons butter
½ cup orange marmalade
½ cup sour cream

Separate eggs. Beat yolks until thick and lemon-colored. Beat in ½ cup of sour cream and salt. Beat eggs whites until stiff but not dry. Fold whites into yolk mixture. Melt butter in a large skillet and pour in egg mixture. Cook over very low heat about 10 minutes or until lightly browned on the bottom. Place pan in a moderate oven (350°F) 10 to 15 minutes or until top is dry and springs back when touched with a finger. Loosen and slide onto a warm plate. Cut into wedges and serve with a mixture made of the marmalade and remaining sour cream. Serves 4 or 5.

2½ cups cooked or canned tomatoes
½ cup chopped green pepper
1 medium onion, chopped
½ cup chopped celery
1 teaspoon sugar
¾ teaspoon salt
⅛ teaspoon pepper
1 matzo, broken*
4 eggs
Salt and pepper
½ cup grated American cheese

SPANISH EGG SURPRISE

Combine tomatoes, green pepper, onion, celery, sugar, salt, and pepper. Bring to a boil and cook 10 minutes. Add broken matzo and place in 1-quart baking dish. Break eggs on top. Sprinkle with salt and pepper; cover with grated cheese. Bake in a moderate oven (350°F) about 20 minutes or until eggs are firm and cheese melted. If desired, bake in 4 individual baking dishes. Serves 4.

*¾ cup matzo farfel may be used instead.

MATZO-MEAL OMELET

6 eggs
½ teaspoon salt
Dash pepper
¾ cup water
¾ cup matzo meal
3 tablespoons butter
Preserves (optional)

Beat eggs until yolks and whites are combined. Add salt, pepper, water, and matzo meal. Heat butter in a large skillet; add egg mixture. Cook over low heat without stirring, lifting with spatula frequently to let uncooked eggs run underneath. When browned on bottom and firm throughout, make a 2-inch cut on either side of the omelet where it will be folded. Using broad spatula, gently fold in half; slide onto platter; serve immediately. Spread with preserves, if desired, before folding. Serves 4 to 6.

LIGHT-AS-A-FEATHER OMELET

6 eggs, separated
½ teaspoon salt
¼ cup potato starch
⅛ teaspoon pepper
⅓ cup water
11-ounce can tomato-and-mushroom sauce, heated

Preheat oven to 350°F. Grease two 9-inch glass pie pans; heat them for a few minutes in the oven before using. Beat egg whites with the salt until stiff but not dry. Beat egg yolks until thick. Add potato starch, pepper, and water; beat until smooth. Fold in beaten egg whites gently but thoroughly. Spread evenly in heated pie pans. Bake at 350°F for 15 minutes or until set. Turn one of the pans out on a serving plate; pour half the heated sauce over the top; turn other pan out on top of this and pour the balance of the sauce over the omelet. Serves 4 to 6.

CREAM-CHEESE SCRAMBLED EGGS

4 ounces cream cheese
2 tablespoons butter
6 eggs
6 tablespoons milk
½ teaspoon salt
¼ teaspoon pepper

Cut cream cheese into ½-inch cubes. Melt butter in a large skillet. Beat eggs with milk, salt, and pepper. Stir in cream cheese. Pour into the skillet and cook over low heat, stirring constantly, until eggs are set. Serves 3 or 4.

DENVER SANDWICHES

6 eggs
½ cup condensed clear chicken soup, undiluted
¼ cup finely chopped onion
¼ cup finely chopped green pepper
2 frankfurters, finely chopped
¼ teaspoon salt
Dash pepper
Pareve margarine or chicken fat
6 Passover Rolls (page 172)

Beat eggs and chicken soup together until well mixed. Stir in onion, green pepper, frankfurters, salt, and pepper. Heat a small amount of the margarine or fat in a small skillet. Pour in about ½ cup of the mixture and cook over low heat until set. If desired, turn and brown on other side. Fold in half and serve on a warm Passover roll (page 172). Repeat until six sandwiches are made.

SAVORY EGGS AND FRANKFURTERS

½ pound frankfurters
¾ cup canned tomato-and-mushroom sauce
1 tablespoon chopped parsley
4 or 8 eggs

Cut frankfurters crosswise into ¼-inch slices. Arrange on bottom of 4 individual baking dishes or in a 1-quart baking dish. Mix tomato-and-mushroom sauce with parsley; spoon over frankfurters. Break 1 or 2 eggs on top for each serving. Bake in a moderate oven (350°F) 20 minutes or until eggs are firm. Serves 4.

NEPTUNE EGG SCRAMBLE

1-pound jar gefilte fish
¾ cup chopped onion
¼ cup butter
8 eggs, beaten
½ cup milk
1 tablespoon lemon juice
¾ teaspoon salt
⅛ teaspoon pepper

Remember fried lox, onions, and eggs? This dish is very similar.

Mash fish with a fork. Sauté onion in butter until tender but not brown. Mix eggs with milk, lemon juice, salt, pepper, and fish. Add to onion mixture and cook over low heat, stirring frequently, until eggs are firm. Serves 6.

FRIED FILLETS OF FLOUNDER

1½ cups (approximately) matzo meal
1 teaspoon salt
⅛ teaspoon pepper
2 eggs beaten with 2 tablespoons cold water
2 pounds flounder fillets
Peanut oil

Combine matzo meal, salt, and pepper. Roll fillets in seasoned matzo meal, dip into egg mixture, and roll again in matzo meal. Do this at least one-half hour before frying and the coating will adhere well. Fry in one-half inch of hot fat in a large skillet. Drain on absorbent paper. Serves 4 to 6.

CRUNCHY POTATO-FRIED FISH

6-ounce package potato-pancake mix
½ cup matzo meal
½ teaspoon salt
2 eggs
2 tablespoons water
2 pounds fish fillets
Peanut oil or vegetable shortening

Mix potato-pancake mix, matzo meal, and salt. Combine eggs and water. Roll fish in potato-pancake mixture, dip in egg mixture, and roll again in potato-pancake mixture. Set aside for at least one-half hour before frying. This makes coating adhere well. Fry in one-half inch hot oil or vegetable shortening in a large skillet. Drain on absorbent paper. Serves 4 to 6.

CHEESE-FRIED FISH

2 eggs
2 tablespoons water
1½ cups matzo meal
1 cup grated American cheese
1 teaspoon salt
Dash pepper
2 pounds fish fillets
Oil or vegetable shortening

Combine eggs and water. Combine matzo meal, cheese, salt, and pepper. Roll fillets in meal mixture, dip in egg mixture, and roll again in meal mixture. Set aside for at least one-half hour before frying. This makes coating adhere well. Fry in one-half inch hot oil or vegetable shortening in a large skillet. Drain on absorbent paper. Serves 4 to 6.

BAKED FISH AND VEGETABLES

6 fish steaks
2 large onions, sliced thin
6 tablespoons butter or pareve margarine
Salt and pepper
11-ounce can tomato-and-mushroom sauce
1 cup diced celery, cooked
2 cups sliced carrots, cooked
4 cups diced potatoes, cooked

Arrange onions on bottom of large baking pan. Place fish steaks on top of onions; dot with 2 tablespoons of the butter or margarine. Sprinkle with salt and pepper. Pour on tomato-and-mushroom sauce. Bake in a hot oven (400°F) 15 minutes. Add well-drained vegetables. Dot with remaining butter or margarine. Bake 20 minutes longer, basting occasionally. Serves 6.

FISH FILLETS AMANDINE

2 pounds fish fillets
½ cup cake meal or matzo meal
1½ teaspoons salt
Dash pepper
3 tablespoons peanut oil
3 tablespoons butter
½ cup blanched, slivered almonds

Roll fish in a mixture of the meal, salt, and pepper. Heat the oil and butter in a large skillet. Fry fish until browned on both sides, about 5 minutes to a side. Remove fish and keep warm. Fry almonds in the remaining fat until lightly browned. Add additional butter if necessary. Serve over fish. Serves 6.

FISH-AND-EGG CASSEROLE

1 large onion, sliced thin
¼ cup butter or pareve margarine
2½ cups matzo farfel*
1-pound jar gefilte fish or Fishlets (drain and save liquid)
3 hard-cooked eggs, sliced**
1½ cups cooked, sliced carrots
1 cup cooked, diced celery
11-ounce can tomato-and-mushroom sauce
¾ cup liquid from gefilte fish
½ cup liquid from vegetables
½ teaspoon salt
Dash white pepper

Sauté onion in butter until tender but not brown. If gefilte fish is used, cut into bite-sized pieces. Arrange matzo farfel, fish, sliced eggs, onions, and vegetables in alternate layers in a greased 2-quart baking dish or 6 individual baking dishes. Combine tomato-and-mushroom sauce with fish liquid, vegetable liquid, salt, and pepper. Pour over top of casserole. Bake in a hot oven (425°F) 15 to 20 minutes or until hot. Serves 6.

*4 matzos, finely broken, may be used instead.

**If desired, eggs may be omitted and a 2-pound jar of gefilte fish used instead of 1 pound.

BUSY-DAY FISH BAKE

6-ounce (or two 3-ounce) package potato-pancake mix
2 eggs
2 cups water
2-pound jar gefilte fish
¼ cup peanut oil or melted butter
¼ cup (1 ounce) grated American cheese

Combine potato-pancake mix with eggs and water as directed on package. Drain and mash gefilte fish. When potato mixture is thickened, stir in the oil or butter and the mashed fish. Spread in a greased 8-inch-square pan; sprinkle with cheese. Bake in a moderate oven (350°F) 30 minutes or until lightly browned at edges. Serves 6.

"OTHER MEALS" MAIN DISHES

YOM TOV FISH MOUSSE

2-pound jar gefilte fish
1 cup chopped walnuts
1 cup sweet cream
1¼ cups matzo meal
¼ cup melted butter
¼ cup lemon juice
½ teaspoon onion powder
1 teaspoon salt
Dash pepper
6 eggs, separated
11-ounce can tomato-and-mushroom sauce

Drain fish and mash in a large bowl. Mix in nuts, cream, matzo meal, butter, lemon juice, onion powder, salt, and pepper. Beat egg yolks and fold in. Beat egg whites until stiff but not dry. Fold into fish mixture. Place in well-greased loaf pan or 9-inch tube pan and spread evenly. Cover pan with aluminum foil. Bake in a moderate oven (350°F) until set and firm to the touch, about 1½ hours. Loosen sides with knife, allow to set for a few minutes, and turn out on serving platter. Serve with heated tomato-and-mushroom sauce. Serves 6 to 8.

GEFILTE-FISH SAUTÉ

2-pound jar gefilte fish
1 egg
1 tablespoon water
¾ cup matzo meal
Butter or pareve margarine

This is one of those dishes that are ridiculously easy to prepare and absolutely marvelous.

Drain fish. Combine egg and water. Dip fish in egg mixture. Roll in matzo meal. Sauté in a small amount of butter or margarine until golden brown on all sides. Serve with Dill Sauce. Serves 4.

DILL SAUCE

½ cup sour cream
¼ cup chopped kosher dill pickles
1 tablespoon pickle juice
¼ teaspoon salt

Combine all ingredients and store in refrigerator until ready to serve. This sauce is best prepared several hours before serving.

SAVORY FISH IN POTATO NESTS

1-pound jar gefilte fish
¾ cup grated American cheese
1 tablespoon lemon juice
1 small onion, minced
3 cups mashed potatoes
¼ cup matzo meal
1 egg, beaten
3 tablespoons butter
1 teaspoon salt
⅛ teaspoon pepper
4 to 6 tomato slices

Drain and mash gefilte fish. Add ½ cup of the grated cheese, lemon juice, and onion. Combine mashed potatoes with matzo meal, egg, butter, salt, and pepper. Form 4 to 6 nests of mashed-potato mixture by dropping mounds onto a greased baking sheet and making an indentation in each with a spoon. Fill with fish mixture. Top with tomato slice; sprinkle with rest of cheese. Bake in moderate oven (350°F) 30 minutes or until browned. Serves 4 to 6.

FISHERMAN'S POTATO PANCAKES

2-pound jar gefilte fish
4 or 5 large raw potatoes, peeled (2 cups when grated)
1 medium onion
3 eggs, slightly beaten
½ cup matzo meal
1 teaspoon salt
¼ teaspoon pepper
Peanut oil

Mash fish with a fork. Grate potatoes and onion or put through food grinder, using fine blade. Mix all 7 ingredients. Drop by tablespoons into hot peanut oil which is almost deep enough to cover pancakes. Fry over moderate heat until browned on one side. Turn; brown other side. Drain on absorbent paper. Serve with sour cream or applesauce. Makes 24.

GOURMET SALMON LOAF

1 pound (2 cups) canned or cooked salmon (drain and save liquid)
⅓ cup salmon liquid
1 cup matzo meal
¾ cup milk
2 eggs, well beaten
½ teaspoon salt
⅛ teaspoon pepper
2 tablespoons melted butter
¼ cup chopped celery
¼ cup minced onion
½ cup coarsely chopped walnuts
2 teaspoons lemon juice
11-ounce can tomato-and-mushroom sauce

Flake salmon; add salmon liquid, matzo meal, milk, eggs, salt, pepper, butter, celery, onion, nuts, and lemon juice. Pack evenly into a well-greased loaf pan, lined on the bottom with waxed paper. Bake in a moderate oven (375°F) 40 minutes or until firm and lightly browned. Serve with heated tomato-and-mushroom sauce. Serves 6.

---

1 pound (2 cups) canned or cooked salmon, drained
⅓ cup salmon liquid
1 cup matzo meal
¾ cup milk
2 eggs, well beaten
½ teaspoon salt
⅛ teaspoon pepper
¼ cup minced parsley
1 tablespoon lemon juice
½ cup minced onion
11-ounce can tomato-and-mushroom sauce

SALMON LOAF

Flake salmon; add salmon liquid, matzo meal, milk, eggs, salt, pepper, parsley, lemon juice, and onion. Pack evenly into a well-greased loaf pan which has been lined on the bottom with waxed paper. Bake in a moderate oven (375°F) 40 minutes or until firm and browned. Serve with heated tomato-and-mushroom sauce. Serves 6.

SALMON CUTLETS

1 pound (2 cups) canned or cooked salmon
½ teaspoon salt
Dash pepper
¼ cup matzo meal
¼ cup minced onion
3 eggs
1 tablespoon water
½ cup matzo meal, for coating
11-ounce can tomato-and-mushroom sauce

Drain and flake salmon. Add salt, pepper, ¼ cup matzo meal, onion, and 2 beaten eggs. Mix well; shape into 6 cutlets. Beat third egg with the water. Dip cutlets in egg mixture, then in the ½ cup of matzo meal. Fry in one inch of hot fat until browned on both sides. Serve with heated tomato-and-mushroom sauce. Serves 3 or 4.

SIMPLE SALMON CASSEROLE

6-ounce (or two 3-ounce) package potato-pancake mix
2 eggs
2 cups water
¼ cup peanut oil or melted butter
1 pound canned or cooked salmon (2 cups)
¼ cup grated American cheese

Combine potato-pancake mix with eggs and water, as directed on package. When thickened, stir in oil or butter and the drained, flaked salmon. Spread in a greased 8-inch-square pan; sprinkle with cheese. Bake in a moderate oven (350°F) 30 minutes. Serves 6.

BUTTERY LEMON SAUCE

2 lemons
2 tablespoons butter or margarine
1 tablespoon potato starch
¼ teaspoon salt
1 cup cold water
1 teaspoon sugar

Peel one lemon; discard rind; slice as thin as possible. Remove seeds. Squeeze juice from second lemon. Melt the butter or margarine in a small saucepan. Combine potato starch and salt. Gradually add water and stir until smooth. Add to melted fat and cook over low heat, stirring constantly, until slightly thickened. Add lemon juice, slices, and sugar. Heat. Serve on broiled or baked fish. Serves 4 to 6.

WINE-BUTTER SAUCE

1 medium onion, diced
3 tablespoons butter
3 tablespoons lemon juice
½ cup catsup
½ cup medium-dry Concord wine

Sauté onion in butter until tender. Add lemon juice, catsup, and wine. Stir and cook briskly about 15 minutes or until sauce is concentrated to measure one cup. Pour over hot broiled fish steaks or fillets. Serves 4 to 6.

MATZO-CHEESE KUGEL

6 matzos, broken into large pieces
5 eggs
1 cup milk
1 pound cottage cheese
1 teaspoon salt
¼ cup sugar
1 teaspoon cinnamon
3 tablespoons melted butter

Beat eggs with milk. Combine thoroughly with cottage cheese, salt, sugar, cinnamon, and melted butter. In a greased 1½-quart baking dish, arrange half the matzo. Pour half the cheese mixture over it. Repeat with balance of matzo and cheese mixture. Bake in a moderate oven (350°F) 40 minutes or until set. Serve with sour cream if desired. Serves 6.

POTATO-CHEESE KUGEL

3 eggs
2 cups water
6-ounce package potato-pancake mix
1 pound cottage cheese
¾ cup sour cream
2 teaspoons minced parsley
Sour cream for topping

Combine eggs, water, and potato-pancake mix as directed on package. After it thickens for 2 minutes, stir in cottage cheese, sour cream, and parsley. Pour into a greased 8-inch-square pan. Bake in a moderate oven (350°F) one hour or until edges begin to brown. Serve topped with sour cream. Serves 6.

CHEESE-MUSHROOM PUFF

½ pound fresh mushrooms, sliced
2 tablespoons butter
2 cups milk
8 ounces American cheese, grated
½ teaspoon salt
Dash pepper
3 eggs, separated
4 matzos, broken*

Sauté mushrooms in butter. Heat milk to just below boiling; stir in cheese, salt, and pepper. Beat egg yolks well; add cheese mixture. Beat egg whites until stiff but not dry; fold into cheese mixture. Mix broken matzos with mushrooms. Fold into cheese mixture. Pour into a greased 12×7½×1½-inch baking dish. Place in a 375°F oven and bake 30 minutes or until a knife inserted in center comes out clean. Serves 4 to 6.

*2¾ cups matzo farfel may be used instead.

ORIENTAL EGGPLANT CASSEROLE

3 tablespoons peanut oil or melted butter
1 large onion, sliced thin
1 medium eggplant (1½ pounds)
¼ cup diced green pepper
11-ounce can tomato-and-mushroom sauce
1 teaspoon salt
¼ teaspoon pepper
2 large tomatoes, peeled and cut into cubes
1 pound cottage cheese
1½ cups matzo farfel*

Sauté onion in fat until tender. Pare eggplant and cut into ½-inch cubes. Combine onion, eggplant, green pepper, tomato-and-mushroom sauce, salt, and pepper. Cover and cook 15 minutes or until eggplant is tender. Stir in tomatoes. In a greased 2-quart baking dish, arrange alternate layers of the vegetables, cheese, and matzo farfel, beginning and ending with the vegetables. Bake, uncovered, in a moderate oven (350°F) 20 minutes. Serves 6.

*Two matzos, finely broken, may be used instead.

MATZO BREI

3 matzos
Butter
2 eggs
2 tablespoons water or milk
¼ teaspoon salt
Dash pepper

Break matzos into pieces. Cover with water and then pour water off immediately. Press excess water out of matzos. Melt about 2 tablespoons of butter in a skillet; add matzos and fry until lightly toasted. Beat eggs with remaining ingredients. Pour over matzos and fry, stirring frequently, until eggs are set. Serves 2 or 3.

FRIED THINGS

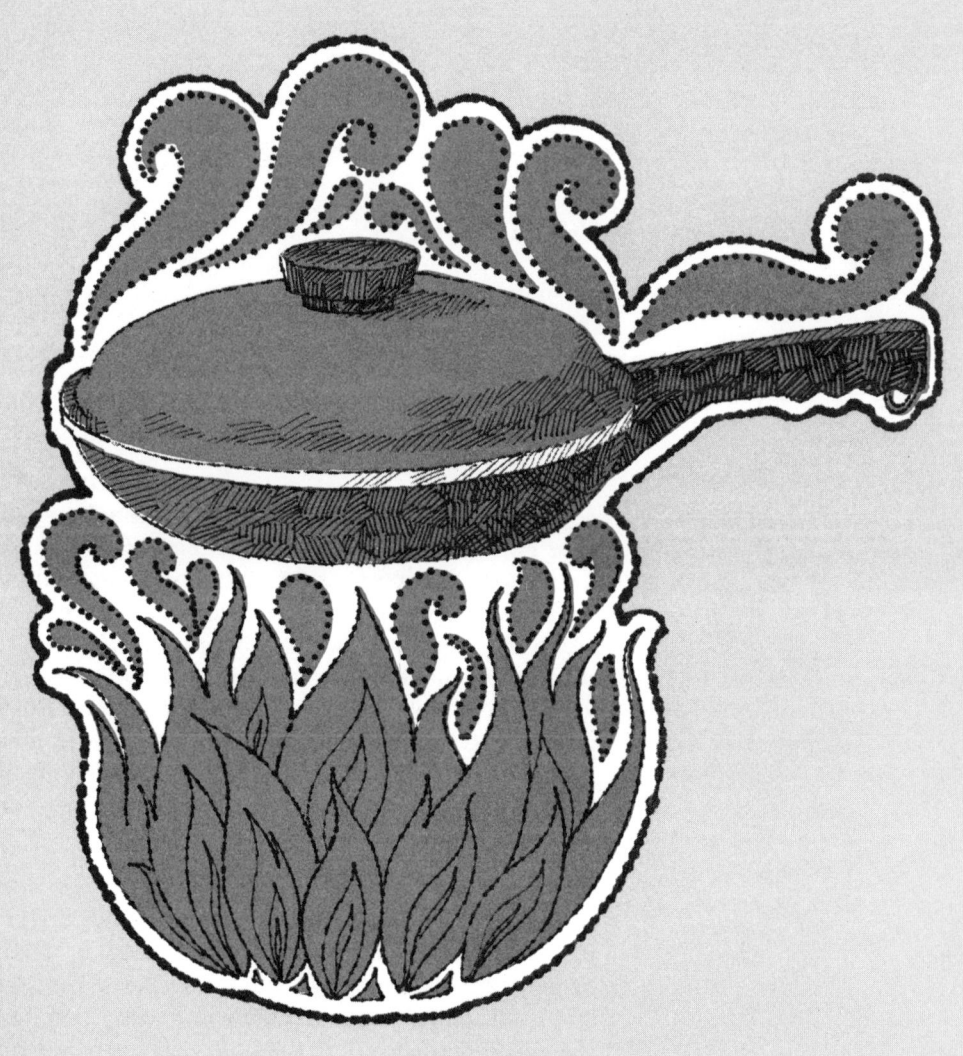

FRIED THINGS

Fried foods need not be indigestible for people who have no special medical problems, if a few basic rules are followed:

1. The fat used should be one that can be heated very hot without smoking. High temperature is necessary to prevent excess fat absorption and resultant sogginess. However, if the fat smokes before it can reach the required heat, it breaks down, and the results are unpleasant. The best fats to use for frying are vegetable oil or vegetable shortening. Butter gives unparalleled flavor but it does smoke at a low temperature. Therefore, it should be used only for brief cooking procedures, like browning foods and scrambling eggs.

2. There are two basic types of frying. To sauté means to cook in a small amount of fat in a frying pan. Deep-fat frying means to cook food in a deep layer of fat, at least high enough to cover the food, and often higher. Each recipe will specify how deep the fat should be. If it says "Fry in deep hot oil," fill the frying kettle or pot no more than two-thirds full or it may foam over and cause a dandy fire.

FRIED THINGS 107

For deep-fat frying, use a deep, straight-sided pot fitted with a wire basket. A frying thermometer is a big help. The traditional bread-browning test for oil heat cannot be used at Passover, of course, so try a small portion of the food to be fried. The fat should sizzle and bubble moderately when the food is introduced.

Do not try to deep-fat-fry too many pieces at the same time, or the oil temperature will drop too low and foods will become soggy and not puff up properly.

3. Always remember to drain fried foods thoroughly on absorbent paper.

PAREVE
⅔ cup cake meal
½ teaspoon salt
1½ cups water
3 eggs

FLEISHIGE
⅔ cup cake meal
½ teaspoon salt
¼ cup water
10½-ounce can condensed clear chicken soup, undiluted
3 eggs

BATTER FOR BLINTZES

Combine cake meal and salt. Combine eggs and liquid. Gradually add the egg mixture to the cake-meal mixture, beating thoroughly to prevent lumps. Allow air bubbles to settle before starting to fry batter. Pour about 3 tablespoons of batter onto a hot, lightly greased frying pan or griddle and rotate to form an 8-inch pancake. Fry until batter sets and curls at the edges. Turn out on a clean cloth, fried-side-up. Makes about 16.

CHEESE BLINTZES

1 recipe Pareve Blintz Batter (page 107)
1 pound cottage cheese
1 egg
½ teaspoon salt
¼ cup sugar
¼ teaspoon cinnamon

Combine cottage cheese, egg, salt, sugar, and cinnamon. Place a heaping tablespoon of filling on the center of each pancake. Fold in the side edges and roll. Fry in a small quantity of peanut oil or butter until browned on both sides. Serve with sour cream.

STRAWBERRIES-AND-CREAM BLINTZES

1 recipe Pareve Blintz Batter (page 107)
1 pound small-curd cottage cheese
1 egg
½ teaspoon salt
¼ cup sugar
¼ teaspoon cinnamon
½ cup sliced strawberries

Mix cheese, egg, salt, sugar, cinnamon, and strawberries. Place a tablespoon of filling in the center of each pancake. Fold in side edges and roll. Fry in a small amount of oil or butter until browned on all sides. Serve with Strawberry Sauce. Makes 12 to 14.

Strawberry Sauce: Combine 1 cup sour cream, 1 cup sliced strawberries, 2 tablespoons sugar. Chill.

SURPRISE BLINTZES

1 recipe Pareve Blintz Batter (page 107)
1 pound cottage cheese
1 egg, beaten
½ teaspoon salt
2 tablespoons sugar
⅓ cup raspberry preserves

Mix cheese with egg, salt, and sugar. Place a tablespoon of filling in the center of each pancake. Top with a little of the preserves. Fold in side edges and roll. Fry in a little peanut oil or butter until browned on all sides. Serve with sour cream. Makes 12 to 14.

FRIED THINGS

FRUIT-NUT-CHEESE BLINTZES

1 recipe Pareve Blintz Batter (page 107)
1 pound cottage cheese
1 egg, slightly beaten
½ teaspoon salt
3 tablespoons sugar
¼ teaspoon cinnamon
¾ cup well-drained fruit cocktail
¼ cup chopped walnuts

Mix the cottage cheese with the next 6 ingredients to make filling. Place a heaping tablespoon of the filling in the center of each pancake. Fold in side edges and roll. Fry in a small amount of peanut oil or butter until browned on both sides. Top with sauce and serve. Makes 16.

Sauce: Mix 1½ cups sour cream with 1 cup well-drained fruit cocktail and 1 tablespoon sugar.

VEGETABLE-CHEESE BLINTZES

1 recipe Pareve Blintz Batter (page 107)
¼ pound mushrooms, sliced
1 large onion, diced
½ cup diced green pepper
¼ cup butter or margarine
1 pound cottage cheese
½ teaspoon salt
1 egg, slightly beaten

Sauté vegetables in hot butter or margarine until tender. Mix with cheese, salt, and egg. Place a heaping tablespoon of the filling in the center of each pancake. Fold in side edges and roll. Fry in a small amount of peanut oil or butter until browned on both sides. Top with sour cream and serve. Makes 16.

LIVER BLINTZES WITH TOMATO-AND-MUSHROOM SAUCE

1 recipe Fleishige Blintz Batter (page 107)
2½ cups (1¼ pounds) broiled, ground liver
2 large onions, minced and sautéed in 3 tablespoons chicken fat or pareve margarine
1 egg, slightly beaten
1 teaspoon salt
Pinch pepper
11-ounce can tomato-and-mushroom sauce

Where is it written that blintzes must be made from just cheese or fruit? Dozens of fillings are possible. This recipe presents an unusual way to serve liver.

Mix liver, sautéed onions, egg, salt, and pepper. Place a heaping tablespoon of filling in the center of each pancake. Fold in side edges and roll tightly. Fry until golden brown in a small amount of chicken fat or pareve margarine. Serve with heated tomato-and-mushroom sauce. Makes 14 to 16.

MEAT BLINTZES

1 recipe Fleishige Blintz Batter (page 107)
1 large onion, minced
3 tablespoons diced green pepper
½ cup diced celery
3 tablespoons chicken fat or pareve margarine
2½ cups ground, cooked meat
1 egg, slightly beaten
11-ounce can tomato-and-mushroom sauce

Sauté vegetables in the fat until tender. Combine with meat and egg. Place a heaping tablespoon of the filling in the center of each pancake. Fold in side edges and roll. Fry in a small amount of peanut oil or pareve margarine until browned on both sides. Top with heated tomato-and-mushroom sauce and serve. Makes 16.

CHICKEN-SALAD BLINTZES

1 recipe Fleishige Blintz Batter (page 107)
2½ cups diced chicken*
½ cup finely diced celery
1 small onion, diced
6 tablespoons mayonnaise
Salt and pepper to taste

Mix chicken or turkey with celery, onion, mayonnaise, salt, and pepper. Place a heaping tablespoon of this filling in the center of each pancake. Fold in side edges and roll. Fry in a small amount of peanut oil or pareve margarine until browned on both sides. Top with Hot Cranberry Sauce and serve. Makes 16.

Hot Cranberry Sauce: Mix together 1-pound can cranberry sauce and 2 tablespoons water. Stir and cook over low heat until hot and smooth.

*Turkey may be used instead.

CHICKEN BLINTZES WITH HOT CRANBERRY SAUCE

1 recipe Fleishige Blintz Batter (page 107)
2½ cups diced cooked chicken*
2 eggs
1 medium onion, diced and sautéed in 1 tablespoon chicken fat or pareve margarine
½ teaspoon salt
Dash pepper
1 recipe Hot Cranberry Sauce (page 110)

Mix chicken with eggs, sautéed onion, salt, and pepper. Place a heaping tablespoon of filling in the center of each pancake. Fold in side edges and roll. Fry until golden brown in a small amount of chicken fat or pareve margarine. Serve with Hot Cranberry Sauce. Makes 16.

*Turkey may be used instead.

MATZO-MEAL LATKES

½ cup matzo meal
¾ teaspoon salt
1 tablespoon sugar
¾ cup cold water
3 eggs

Combine matzo meal, salt, and sugar. Separate the eggs. Beat yolks slightly and combine with the water. Add the liquid to the dry ingredients. Allow to stand for 15 to 20 minutes. Beat the egg whites until stiff. Fold them into the matzo-meal mixture. Drop by tablespoonsful onto a hot, well-greased frying pan or griddle and brown on both sides. Makes 10 to 12.

POTATO LATKES

2 cups (4 or 5 large) grated raw potatoes
1 medium onion
2 eggs
1½ teaspoons salt
Dash pepper
¼ cup matzo meal

Pare vegetables and grate or put through a meat grinder, using the fine blade. Add eggs, salt, pepper, and matzo meal. Drop by tablespoonsful into hot peanut oil almost deep enough to cover the pancakes. Fry over moderate heat until browned on one side. Turn and brown other side. Drain on absorbent paper. Serves 4.

WHITE-AND-GOLD POTATO LATKES

2 large white potatoes (1 cup grated)
1 large sweet potato (1 cup grated)
1 medium onion
2 eggs
1½ teaspoons salt
Dash pepper
¼ cup matzo meal
Peanut oil

Pare vegetables and grate or put through a meat grinder, using the fine blade. Add eggs, salt, pepper, and matzo meal. Drop by tablespoonsful into hot peanut oil almost deep enough to cover the pancakes. Fry over moderate heat until browned on one side. Turn and brown other side. Drain on absorbent paper. Serves 4.

COCONUT LATKES

3 eggs, separated
¾ teaspoon salt
½ cup matzo meal
¾ cup cold water
1 tablespoon sugar
¾ cup shredded coconut

Beat egg yolks with salt and water. Add matzo meal, sugar, and coconut. Allow to stand for 15 to 20 minutes. Beat egg whites until stiff. Fold them into the matzo-meal mixture. Drop by tablespoonful onto a hot, well-greased frying pan or griddle and brown on both sides over low heat. Serve with sour cream. Makes 18.

CHEESE LATKES

3 eggs, well beaten
1 cup milk
1 cup pot cheese
1 cup matzo meal
¾ teaspoon salt
½ teaspoon cinnamon
1 tablespoon sugar

Beat together the eggs, milk, and cheese. Combine the remaining ingredients and add to egg mixture; blend well. Drop by tablespoonsful onto a hot, well-greased frying pan or griddle and brown on both sides. Serve hot with sour cream, applesauce, or preserves. Makes 16.

SALAMI LATKES

3 eggs
1 teaspoon salt
¾ cup water
1 tablespoon sugar
1 cup matzo meal
1 cup diced salami (about ¼ pound)*

Combine eggs, salt, water, and sugar. Add matzo meal; mix well; fold in salami. Drop by tablespoonsful into ½-inch-deep fat and fry until golden brown. Drain on absorbent paper. Serve with applesauce. Makes 10.

*Sliced frankfurters may be used instead.

LUNCHEON LATKES

½ cup chopped onion
2 tablespoons fat
3 eggs, beaten
1 teaspoon salt
¾ cup water
1 tablespoon sugar
1½ cups chopped, cooked meat
1¼ cups matzo meal

Also delicious cold, these latkes can be taken to school or work for lunch.

Sauté onions in fat until tender. Combine eggs, salt, water, and sugar. Add onions, meat, and matzo meal. Drop by tablespoonsful into 1-inch-deep hot fat and fry until golden brown. Drain on absorbent paper. Serve hot with applesauce or meat gravy. Makes 8.

FISHLET CROQUETTES

½ cup matzo meal
2 cups mashed potatoes
2 eggs, slightly beaten
1½ teaspoons salt
⅛ teaspoon white pepper
1-pound jar Fishlets
1 egg, beaten with 1 tablespoon of water
Matzo meal
Peanut oil

Combine thoroughly the first 5 ingredients. With wet hands, shape tablespoons of this mixture into balls. Make a depression in the center of each ball, place a Fishlet inside, and cover the opening. Dip each one in the egg mixture and then roll in matzo meal. Fry in deep, hot peanut oil (375°F) until golden brown. Serves 6.

DELECTABLE CHEESE CROQUETTES

2 cups cottage cheese, drained
2 cups mashed potatoes, cooled
2 eggs, well beaten
½ cup minced onion
1 teaspoon salt
¼ teaspoon pepper
1½ cups matzo meal
2 eggs, beaten with 2 tablespoons water

Combine first 6 ingredients. Chill in refrigerator. Shape into rolls 3 inches long and 1 inch in diameter. Roll in matzo meal, then in egg mixture, and again in matzo meal. Chill in refrigerator at least one hour. Fry in deep, hot oil (375°F) until golden brown. Drain on absorbent paper. Serve with sour cream or applesauce. Serves 6.

APPLE FRITTERS

1 cup matzo meal
3 eggs, beaten
1 teaspoon salt
¾ cup water
2 medium tart apples, peeled and chopped
2 tablespoons sugar
1 teaspoon cinnamon

Combine eggs, salt, and water. Add to matzo meal. Add apples, sugar, and cinnamon; blend well. Drop by tablespoonsful into 1-inch-deep hot fat and fry until golden brown. Drain on absorbent paper. Sprinkle with cinnamon and sugar. Serve with sour cream. Makes 12 to 14.

BANANA FRITTERS

3 eggs, beaten
1 teaspoon salt
¾ cup water
2 tablespoons sugar
1 teaspoon cinnamon
1¼ cups matzo meal
2 large, firm bananas, sliced

Combine eggs, salt, water, sugar, and cinnamon. Add matzo meal and mix well. Fold in bananas. Drop by tablespoonsful into 1-inch-deep hot fat and fry until golden brown. Drain on absorbent paper. Serve with sour cream. Makes 12.

SALADS, DRESSINGS, AND RELISHES

SALADS, DRESSINGS, AND RELISHES

Years ago, even when many Jewish immigrants had very little money, the women insisted on serving the customary salad platter, which in the wintertime meant extravagantly priced lettuce, cucumbers, and hothouse tomatoes, at least for Shabbat and Yom Tov. Nothing else would do.

Fortunately, today, people are more flexible. Salad can be made of many different ingredients, the more crisp and colorful, the better. There is nothing wrong with a lettuce, tomato, and cucumber salad, but why not prepare all the vegetables in chunks and toss in a bowl with a flavorful dressing? Or if tomatoes and cucumbers are outrageously expensive, what's wrong with crisp mixed greens or cole slaw? Use your imagination and remember the cardinal rule—all ingredients must be crisp, chilled, and well drained.

Some of the salads are meant for main courses for light meals. You'll recognize them.

TOSSED LETTUCE AND TOMATOES

½ cup mayonnaise
¼ cup catsup
⅛ teaspoon salt
Dash pepper
Dash garlic powder
2 tablespoons chopped green pepper
1 hard-cooked egg, chopped
1 medium head lettuce
2 medium tomatoes, cut up

Combine mayonnaise, catsup, salt, pepper, garlic powder, green pepper, and egg. Cover and chill for at least one hour. Wash and core lettuce. Tear into bite-size pieces. Toss all ingredients together just before serving. Serves 6 to 8.

---

2 cups sliced, unpeeled cucumbers
¼ cup thinly sliced mild onion
¾ cup thinly sliced red radishes
1 cup sour cream
1 tablespoon sugar
1 tablespoon cider vinegar
Salt and pepper

CUCUMBER SALAD

Combine vegetables. Combine sour cream, sugar, and vinegar. Blend both mixtures; season to taste. Chill. Serve plain or on crisp lettuce. Serves 4 to 6.

---

3 cups grated raw carrot
¾ cup raisins
½ cup nuts, chopped (optional)
Mayonnaise

CARROT-AND-RAISIN SALAD

Mix carrots, raisins, and nuts. Moisten with mayonnaise. Chill; serve on crisp lettuce. Serves 6.

SPECIAL COLE SLAW

½ cup mayonnaise
½ cup sour cream
¼ cup cider vinegar
1½ tablespoons sugar
1 teaspoon salt
Dash pepper
3 cups shredded red cabbage
4 cups shredded green cabbage
2 large unpeeled apples, cored and chopped
½ cup raisins (optional)

Combine mayonnaise, sour cream, vinegar, sugar, salt, and pepper. Mix cabbage, apples, and raisins. Blend with the dressing. Chill several hours before serving. Serves 8.

WALDORF SALAD

½ cup mayonnaise
1 teaspoon sugar
2 cups diced, unpared red apples*
1 cup diced celery
½ cup coarsely chopped walnuts

Blend mayonnaise and sugar. Combine all ingredients; toss thoroughly or apples will turn color. Chill. Serve on crisp lettuce. Serves 4.

*If desired, substitute pared diced pears or use half apples and half pears.

SUPPER WALDORF SALAD

1-pound jar gefilte fish or Fishlets
1 cup diced, unpeeled apple
1 cup thinly sliced celery
¼ cup coarsely chopped walnuts
½ cup mayonnaise

Drain fish. If gefilte fish is used, cut into ¾-inch cubes. Combine all ingredients and mix lightly. Chill. Serve in crisp lettuce cups. Serves 3 or 4.

HEARTY SUPPER SALAD

1-pound jar gefilte fish or Fishlets, drained
2 tablespoons French dressing
2 tablespoons mayonnaise
1 cup sliced celery
2 hard-cooked eggs, diced
¼ cup blanched, slivered almonds

If using gefilte fish, cut into bite-size pieces. Mix the mayonnaise and French dressing. Combine all ingredients and toss lightly. Chill and serve on crisp lettuce. Serves 4 or 5.

FISHLET BOATS

1-pound jar Fishlets, drained
1 cup celery, sliced
½ cup horseradish dressing (see below)
3 6-inch cucumbers

To make the boats, pare the cucumbers. Cut in half lengthwise. Remove seeds and some of the cucumber itself, if necessary, so that shell is ¼-inch thick. Combine Fishlets with the celery and ½ cup of Horseradish Dressing. Fill boats and serve on lettuce. Serve with the balance of the Horseradish Dressing. Serves 3 or 4.

HORSERADISH DRESSING

1 cup commercial sour cream
3 tablespoons vinegar or lemon juice
1 teaspoon salt
2 tablespoons prepared red horseradish

Combine these 4 ingredients and beat thoroughly until well blended.

SNAPPY FISH SALAD

2-pound jar gefilte fish or Fishlets, drained
1 cup sliced celery
½ cup chopped kosher dill pickle
2 large tomatoes, diced
¼ cup mayonnaise
¼ cup buttermilk
2 tablespoons cider vinegar
1 tablespoon sugar
½ teaspoon salt
¼ teaspoon pepper

If gefilte fish is used, cut into bite-size pieces. Combine with celery, pickle, and tomato. Mix mayonnaise, buttermilk, vinegar, sugar, salt, and pepper. Pour over fish mixture and toss lightly. Serve on crisp lettuce. Serves 4 to 6.

MARINER'S COLE SLAW

2-pound jar gefilte fish or Fishlets, drained
⅓ cup mayonnaise
⅓ cup sour cream
½ teaspoon salt
Pinch pepper
3 cups shredded cabbage
¼ cup chopped green pepper
¼ cup finely minced onion
1 large carrot, grated

If gefilte fish is used, cut into bite-size pieces. Combine mayonnaise, sour cream, salt, and pepper. Toss all ingredients together. Serves 4 to 6.

SHICKER'S CHICKEN SALAD

1½ cups diced apples
3 tablespoons Concord-grape wine
3 cups cooked, diced chicken
1½ cups diced celery
1 teaspoon salt
½ cup mayonnaise

Marinate diced apples in the wine. Mix all ingredients and toss gently. Serve on lettuce, garnished with quarters of hard-cooked eggs. Serves 5 to 6.

SALADS, DRESSINGS, AND RELISHES

CRISP-AND-TART CHICKEN SALAD

DRESSING

¾ cup canned condensed clear chicken soup, undiluted
⅓ cup cider vinegar
2 tablespoons sugar
1 tablespoon potato starch
2 egg yolks, beaten

SALAD MIXTURE

4 cups diced, cooked chicken (or turkey)
2 cups diced celery
1 cup small white seedless grapes
½ cup toasted, slivered almonds (optional)

Cook soup, vinegar, sugar, and potato starch over low heat, stirring frequently, until mixture is clear and slightly thickened. Beat this mixture gradually into the beaten egg yolks. Return to pot and cook until thickened (2 to 3 minutes). Cool. When this dressing is completely cooled, combine with salad mixture. Serves 6 to 8.

---

1 cup mayonnaise
½ cup catsup
⅛ teaspoon onion powder
Dash garlic powder

RUSSIAN DRESSING

Combine all ingredients and mix well.

---

1 cup peanut oil
¼ cup Concord-grape wine
3 tablespoons cider vinegar
1 teaspoon salt
¼ teaspoon white pepper
2 tablespoons minced parsley
2 teaspoons sugar

RUBY SALAD DRESSING

Combine in a tightly sealed jar and shake vigorously before serving.

FRENCH DRESSING

⅓ cup cider vinegar
⅔ cup peanut oil
¼ teaspoon pepper
1 teaspoon salt
1 teaspoon sugar (optional)
1 teaspoon paprika

Shake all ingredients in a tightly sealed jar until thoroughly blended. Store in refrigerator until needed.

Garlic French Dressing: Put a clove of garlic in the jar and allow to sit at least 24 hours. Or add ¼ teaspoon garlic powder to ingredients.

Tomato French Dressing: Add ¼ cup catsup.

Horseradish French Dressing: Add 2 tablespoons prepared horseradish.

Lemon French Dressing: Use lemon juice instead of vinegar.

Chiffonade Dressing: Add 1 tablespoon chopped scallions, 2 tablespoons minced green pepper, 1 tablespoon minced parsley, and 2 finely chopped hard-cooked eggs.

SOUR-CREAM DRESSING

1 cup sour cream
¼ cup cider vinegar
1 teaspoon salt
Dash pepper
2 tablespoons sugar
2 tablespoons grated onion

Combine all ingredients and serve on vegetable salads or mixed greens.

CUCUMBER SAUCE FOR GEFILTE FISH

½ cup mayonnaise
2 tablespoons cider vinegar
½ cup sour cream
1 teaspoon scraped onion
1 teaspoon sugar
½ teaspoon salt
Dash pepper
1 cup peeled, finely chopped cucumber
1 tablespoon chopped parsley

Drain chopped cucumber. Stir together mayonnaise and vinegar until smooth. Add remaining ingredients and mix well. Chill until ready to use. Serve on chilled gefilte fish. Makes 2 cups.

SALADS, DRESSINGS, AND RELISHES

ALMOND-CRANBERRY SAUCE

⅓ cup blanched, slivered almonds
1 tablespoon chicken fat or pareve margarine
1-pound can cranberry sauce

Sauté the slivered almonds in the chicken fat in a frying pan until lightly browned, about 5 minutes. Mash cranberry sauce with a fork and stir in toasted nuts. Chill and serve with meat or poultry.

CRANBERRY-CABBAGE RELISH

6 cups finely chopped cabbage
1-pound can cranberry sauce
1 teaspoon salt

Break up cranberry sauce with a fork. Blend with cabbage and salt. Chill in refrigerator for a few hours before serving with meat, poultry, or fish. Serves 6 to 8.

CRANBERRY-APPLE RELISH

1-pound can cranberry sauce
1 cup applesauce

Break up cranberry sauce with a fork. Stir in applesauce and chill. Serve as accompaniment to meat and poultry.

VEGETABLES AND SIDE DISHES

VEGETABLES AND SIDE DISHES

With peas and beans of all kinds prohibited for Pesach, and with the preference of Eastern European Jews often limited to peas, carrots, and string beans, the vegetable story for Passover was rather pathetic years ago. How many times in an eight-day holiday can you eat carrots? Nutrition requirements do not halt at any time of the year, and certainly at this season, when Jews celebrate their liberation from slavery, they should not be abusing themselves in any way. Besides, well-prepared vegetables add texture, color, and flavor to a meal.

Sephardic Jews have used and enjoyed a wide variety of vegetables through the years. Ashkenazim, if they have not done so yet, might decide that now is the time to experiment and explore. A little sauce, a little seasoning, a little spirit of adventure go a long way with vegetables.

VEGETABLES AND SIDE DISHES

SAVORY HONEYED BEETS

3 pounds beets
¾ cup pareve margarine
¾ cup honey
¾ cup catsup
1 tablespoon grated orange rind

Cook and peel beets. Use baby beets if possible; if not, slice large ones after cooking. In a large skillet, combine the margarine, honey, catsup, and orange rind. Bring to a boil, reduce heat, and simmer 5 minutes. Add beets and simmer 10 minutes longer or until glazed. Serves 6 to 8.

BEETS À L'ORANGE

3 cups sliced, cooked beets
⅓ cup sugar
1 tablespoon potato starch
½ teaspoon salt
¼ cup beet juice
½ cup orange juice
1 teaspoon grated orange rind
1 tablespoon pareve margarine

Drain beets and save liquid. Combine sugar, potato starch, and salt in a saucepan. Stir in the beet juice. Cook over moderate heat, stirring constantly, until very thick. Add orange juice, orange rind, margarine, and sliced beets. Mix until beets are well coated. Heat thoroughly and serve. Serves 6.

MARMALADE BEETS

4 cups cooked, sliced beets, drained
2 tablespoons lemon juice
1 tablespoon potato starch
½ cup orange marmalade
3 tablespoons pareve margarine
½ teaspoon salt
Dash pepper
⅛ teaspoon ginger

Mix lemon juice with potato starch in a saucepan. Add marmalade and margarine. Heat, stirring constantly, until marmalade and margarine melt. Add seasonings and beets. Stir and heat about 5 minutes or until beets are well coated. Serves 4 to 6.

HARVARD BEETS

3 cups sliced, cooked beets
⅓ cup sugar
1 tablespoon potato starch
½ teaspoon salt
¼ cup cider vinegar
¼ cup beet juice
1 tablespoon vegetable shortening
or pareve margarine

Drain beets and save liquid. Combine sugar, potato starch, and salt in a saucepan. Stir in cider vinegar and beet juice. Cook over moderate heat, stirring constantly, until thickened. Add beets and shortening; mix until all beets are well coated. Heat thoroughly and serve. Serves 6.

DEBORAH'S BRUSSELS SPROUTS

2 pounds brussels sprouts
2 tablespoons pareve margarine or vegetable shortening
6 tablespoons sugar
2 teaspoons potato starch
½ cup cider vinegar
¼ cup chopped onion
⅛ teaspoon ginger
½ cup raisins

Cook sprouts in salted water. Drain; keep warm. Melt the fat. Mix sugar and potato starch; blend in vinegar. Add vinegar mixture, onion, and ginger to the fat. Simmer 5 minutes or until almost thickened. Add raisins and simmer until sauce is thickened and raisins are plump. Pour sauce over sprouts. Serves 6.

SAVORY BRUSSELS SPROUTS

1 quart brussels sprouts
3 tablespoons pareve margarine
½ cup sliced onion
½ cup canned condensed clear chicken soup, undiluted

Boil sprouts in salted water until almost tender. Drain; keep warm. Melt margarine; add onion and cook about 10 minutes or until soft. Add chicken soup. Add sprouts and simmer until tender. Season to taste. Serves 4 to 6.

PIQUANT CARROTS

1 pound carrots
2 tablespoons pareve margarine
2 tablespoons cake meal
½ teaspoon salt
Dash pepper
2 tablespoons sugar
2 tablespoons lemon juice
1 cup hot carrot liquor

Cook carrots and save carrot liquor. Melt margarine; blend in cake meal and brown slightly. Add salt, pepper, and sugar. Gradually stir in lemon juice and carrot liquor. Stir over low heat until slightly thickened and smooth. Pour over cooked carrots and simmer until sauce is thick. Serves 4.

CARROT PUDDING

3 cups grated raw carrots
¾ cup matzo meal
2 eggs, slightly beaten
¼ cup minced onion
1 teaspoon salt
2 tablespoons melted chicken fat or pareve margarine
10½-ounce can condensed clear chicken soup, undiluted
2 teaspoons minced parsley

Combine all ingredients and mix well. Pour into greased 1½-quart baking dish. Bake in a moderate oven (325°F) 50 minutes or until firm. Serves 6.

CARROT TIMBALES

3 cups grated raw carrots
¾ cup matzo meal
2 eggs, slightly beaten
¼ cup minced onion
1 teaspoon salt
2 tablespoons melted chicken fat or pareve margarine
10½-ounce can condensed clear chicken soup, undiluted
2 teaspoons minced parsley

Combine all ingredients and mix well. Fill greased custard cups ⅔ full. Bake in a moderate oven (325°F) 45 minutes or until firm. Loosen edges with knife and unmold. Serve hot. Makes 6.

FRENCH-FRIED CARROTS

12 small whole carrots
1 egg
1 tablespoon water
Matzo meal
Peanut oil
Salt

Boil carrots in salted water until almost tender. Remove skins; dry. Combine egg and water. Roll carrots in matzo meal, then in egg mixture and again in matzo meal. Fry in deep, hot oil (375°F) until golden brown. Drain. Sprinkle with salt if desired. Serves 4.

HONEY-GLAZED CARROTS*

12 small whole carrots or 6 quartered large ones
1½ tablespoons chicken fat or pareve margarine
¼ cup honey

Cook carrots in boiling salted water until tender. Drain thoroughly and then allow to stand a few minutes to dry. In a skillet, blend fat with honey. Add carrots and simmer slowly until browned and glazed, turning frequently.

*Ginger-Honey-Glazed Carrots: Add ½ teaspoon ginger to fat-honey mixture.

LYONNAISE CARROTS

1 pound carrots
10½-ounce can condensed clear chicken soup, undiluted
¼ cup pareve margarine
3 medium onions, sliced
1 tablespoon potato starch
½ teaspoon sugar
Salt and pepper

Pare carrots and cut into julienne strips about 3 inches long. Bring ¾ cup of the soup to a boil; add carrots; cover and cook 10 minutes. Heat margarine in large skillet; add onions; cover and cook over low heat until tender but not brown, stirring occasionally. Dissolve potato starch in a little of the remaining cold chicken soup. Add the balance of the soup and the sugar. Pour over onions and cook until thickened. Add carrots and the soup in which they were cooked. Simmer, uncovered, until carrots are tender, about 15 minutes longer. Season to taste with salt and pepper. Serves 4.

VEGETABLES AND SIDE DISHES

CRUNCHY HARVARD CARROTS

3 cups cooked, sliced carrots
⅓ cup sugar
1 tablespoon potato starch
½ teaspoon salt
¼ cup cider vinegar
¼ cup orange juice
2 tablespoons pareve margarine or vegetable shortening
¼ cup blanched, slivered almonds
⅛ teaspoon ginger

Drain carrots well. Combine sugar, potato starch, and salt in a saucepan. Stir in vinegar and orange juice. Cook over moderate heat, stirring constantly, until thickened. In a skillet, toast almonds in the fat until golden. Add carrots, almonds, and ginger to the sauce; mix until well blended and heated. Serves 6.

CARROT PANCAKES

4 eggs
1 pound carrots, grated
1 teaspoon sugar
1 teaspoon salt
⅛ teaspoon pepper
2 tablespoons chopped parsley
¼ cup chopped onion
½ cup matzo meal
½ cup water
Peanut oil for frying

Beat eggs well; add remaining 8 ingredients. Heat ⅛ inch of oil in a large skillet. Drop mixture into the oil by tablespoonsful, spreading slightly with back of spoon. Fry on both sides until lightly browned. Makes 14 to 16.

YOM TOV CARROT RING

10½-ounce can condensed clear chicken soup
1 soup can water
1 pound carrots, scraped and sliced
1 large onion, sliced
1¼ teaspoons salt
⅛ teaspoon white pepper
3 eggs
½ cup matzo meal

Combine chicken soup and water and bring to a boil. Add carrots and onions; cover tightly and cook until tender. Drain and save the soup. Puree vegetables, using a food mill, medium strainer, or blender. (If blender is used, add a little of the soup to facilitate pureeing.) Add salt and pepper. Beat eggs; add matzo meal; beat well. Gradually add the soup and beat until smooth. Mix this sauce with the pureed vegetables and pour into a well-greased 5-cup ring mold. Bake in a moderate oven (375°F) 45 minutes or until firm. Turn out on a platter and fill center with a cooked green vegetable. Serves 4 to 6.

NEW ORLEANS CAULIFLOWER

1 large head cauliflower
1 medium onion, diced
1 small green pepper, diced
2 stalks celery, diced
3 tablespoons vegetable shortening or pareve margarine
11-ounce can tomato-and-mushroom sauce

Remove leaves and stalks of cauliflower, cut off woody base, and separate into florets. Wash well and cook in salted water until just tender, about 8 minutes. Do not overcook. Keep warm. In a saucepan, combine onion, green pepper, celery, fat, and tomato-and-mushroom sauce. Simmer 15 minutes. Pour over cauliflower. Serves 6.

FRENCH-FRIED CAULIFLOWER

1 medium head cauliflower
¾ cup matzo meal
1 teaspoon salt
1 egg
1 tablespoon water
Oil for deep frying

Separate cauliflower into small florets. Wash and dry thoroughly. Combine matzo meal and salt. Beat egg and water together. Dip cauliflower in beaten egg mixture and then roll in salted matzo meal. Heat oil to 375°F. Place cauliflower in frying basket and cook in oil for about 5 minutes or until golden brown. Drain thoroughly on absorbent paper and serve hot. Serves 4 to 6.

BRAISED CELERY

2 bunches (about 18 large stalks) celery
¼ cup minced onion
¼ cup chopped carrot
10½-ounce can condensed clear chicken soup, undiluted
2 tablespoons melted chicken fat or pareve margarine
1 teaspoon salt
Dash pepper

Wash celery and remove tough outer leaves. Cut stalks crosswise in halves or quarters. Arrange in a greased baking dish with onion and carrot. Add condensed chicken soup, which has been mixed with the melted fat, salt, and pepper. Cover and bake in a moderate oven (375°F) one hour or until tender. If desired, instead of baking, this mixture may be simmered in a saucepan on top of the stove for 20 minutes or until tender. Serves 6.

VEGETABLES AND SIDE DISHES

CELERY AND CARROTS À L'ATHÈNE

1 large bunch (12 to 14 stalks) celery
½ pound carrots, scraped
1 tablespoon potato starch
10½-ounce can condensed clear chicken soup, undiluted
¼ cup lemon juice
¼ teaspoon garlic powder
1 large onion, finely chopped
½ teaspoon salt
Dash pepper
2 slices lemon

Cut celery into ½-inch slices. Slice carrots. Cook until tender. Drain. Mix potato starch with a few spoonsful of the soup and set aside. Combine balance of soup, lemon juice, garlic powder, onion, salt, pepper, and lemon. Bring to a boil and simmer 10 minutes. Stir in potato-starch mixture and add cooked vegetables. Simmer about 5 minutes or until sauce is thickened. Serves 6.

CELERY AND MUSHROOMS AMANDINE

5 cups celery, cut ¼-inch thick
10½-ounce can condensed clear chicken soup, undiluted
½ pound mushrooms, sliced
2 tablespoons chicken fat or pareve margarine
¼ cup toasted, blanched, slivered almonds

Cook celery in chicken soup until tender. Drain. (This broth may be added to a soup or stew.) Sauté mushrooms in fat. Combine celery, mushrooms, and nuts. Serves 4 to 6.

SPANISH EGGPLANT

1 medium-sized eggplant
Salt and pepper
1 egg
1 tablespoon water
Matzo meal
11-ounce can tomato-and-mushroom sauce
¼ cup water

Wash and pare eggplant. Cut into thin circles or any other desired shape. Sprinkle with salt and pepper. Dip in egg beaten with a tablespoon of water, and then in matzo meal. Brown on both sides in a small amount of fat. Drain on absorbent paper. Place in baking dish and add tomato-and-mushroom sauce mixed with ¼ cup water. Bake in a moderate oven (375°F) 30 minutes or until tender. Serves 6.

CREOLE EGGPLANT

1 medium eggplant, peeled and cubed
1 small green pepper, coarsely diced
1 large onion, chopped
11-ounce can tomato-and-mushroom sauce
½ cup water

Put all ingredients in a saucepan and cook one-half hour or until vegetables are tender. Season to taste with salt and pepper. Serves 6.

FRIED EGGPLANT

1 large eggplant
2 eggs, slightly beaten
1½ cups matzo meal
1 teaspoon salt
⅛ teaspoon pepper

Peel eggplant and cut into slices about ½-inch thick. Cut slices into ½-inch sticks. Mix matzo meal with salt and pepper. Dip eggplant sticks into egg and then the seasoned matzo meal. Brown on all sides in a small amount of hot fat. Drain on absorbent paper. Serves 6.

SWEET-AND-SOUR SPINACH

1 pound spinach
2 medium tomatoes
1 large onion, diced
3 tablespoons pareve margarine
2 tablespoons cake meal
¼ cup lemon juice or cider vinegar
2 tablespoons sugar
1 teaspoon salt

Wash spinach, drain, and chop. Peel tomatoes and cut into small pieces. In a 4-quart pot, cook onion in margarine until tender. Add cake meal and stir over very low heat until lightly browned. Blend in lemon juice or vinegar, sugar, and salt until smooth. Add tomatoes and spinach; cover and cook about 10 minutes or until tender, stirring occasionally. Serves 4.

CREAMED SPINACH

3 tablespoons butter
2 cloves garlic
1 small onion, minced
1½ tablespoons potato starch
1 cup milk
1 teaspoon salt
¼ teaspoon pepper
2 pounds spinach, washed, chopped, and cooked

In a saucepan, sauté garlic and onion in the butter until onion is tender. Discard garlic. Gradually add milk to potato starch. Stir in salt and pepper. Slowly add milk mixture to sautéed onions and stir over low heat until thickened. The sauce gets very thick very quickly. Stir in well-drained spinach and heat. Serves 6.

SCALLOPED TOMATOES

2½ cups stewed or canned tomatoes
¼ cup chopped onion
1 teaspoon salt
¼ teaspoon pepper
1 tablespoon sugar
1½ cups matzo farfel
¼ cup melted chicken fat or pareve margarine

Combine first 5 ingredients. Combine matzo farfel with melted fat. In a greased 1-quart baking dish, arrange alternate layers of the farfel mixture and the tomato mixture, beginning and ending with farfel mixture. Bake in a moderate oven (375°F) 30 minutes or until lightly browned on top. Serves 4 to 6.

SCALLOPED POTATOES IN TOMATO SAUCE

2 large onions, sliced thin
3 tablespoons chicken fat, pareve margarine, or butter
6 medium potatoes (2½ pounds)
11-ounce can tomato-and-mushroom sauce
½ teaspoon salt
Dash of pepper

Sauté onions in fat until tender. Cut peeled potatoes into thin slices. Arrange alternate layers of potato and onion in a greased 1½-quart baking dish. Stir salt and pepper into tomato-and-mushroom sauce. Pour over the top and shake dish gently to distribute sauce. Cover and bake in a moderate oven (375°F) one hour or until potatoes are tender. Serves 6.

PRUNE-AND-POTATO TZIMMES

2 tablespoons chicken fat or pareve margarine
½ cup diced onion
2 pounds white potatoes
1¼ teaspoons salt
1 large or 2 small marrow bones
2½ cups liquid (juice from prunes plus water)
¼ cup sugar
1 teaspoon paprika
1 tablespoon lemon juice
1-pound jar stewed prunes

In a heavy 4-quart saucepan, sauté onion in the fat until tender. Peel potatoes; cut into quarters if large; leave whole if small. Put potatoes, salt, marrow bones, prune juice and water, sugar, paprika, and lemon juice in pot with onions. Simmer, uncovered, over low heat for 1¼ hours. Add drained prunes and cook ½ hour longer, stirring occasionally. Serves 6.

POTATOES EN CASSEROLE

4 cups thinly sliced, pared raw potatoes
½ cup minced onion
1 tablespoon potato starch
½ teaspoon salt
⅛ teaspoon pepper
3 tablespoons chicken fat or pareve margarine
10½-ounce can condensed clear chicken soup, undiluted

In a greased 1½-quart casserole, arrange a layer of potatoes. Add some of the onion. Sprinkle with some of the potato starch, salt, and pepper. Dot with some of the fat. Repeat until all ingredients are used, ending with some of the fat on top. Add the chicken soup. Cover and bake in a moderate oven (350°F) 45 minutes. Uncover and bake 15 minutes longer or until tender. Serves 4 to 6.

GOLDEN PARSLEY POTATOES

3 pounds (about 18) small potatoes, peeled
1 cup water
10½-ounce can condensed clear chicken soup, undiluted
1 teaspoon salt
Pinch pepper
½ cup chopped parsley

Bring the condensed chicken soup, water, and seasonings to a boil. Add the peeled, whole potatoes; cover and simmer 15 minutes. Uncover and cook until almost all the liquid is absorbed, basting occasionally. Sprinkle with chopped parsley and toss lightly. Serves 6.

CRUSTY ROASTED POTATOES

8 large baking potatoes, peeled
½ cup chicken fat or pareve margarine
1¼ teaspoons salt
½ cup canned condensed clear chicken soup, undiluted

Melt fat in a baking pan. Roll potatoes in the fat until well coated. Sprinkle with salt. Bake, uncovered, in a moderate oven (350°F) one hour. Turn potatoes. Add condensed soup and bake one hour longer, basting and turning as needed to brown evenly. Serves 8.

SWEET-POTATO-AND-APPLESAUCE PUDDING

6 medium sweet potatoes (3 pounds)
2 cups applesauce
¾ teaspoon cinnamon
¾ cup honey
3 tablespoons melted chicken fat or pareve margarine

Cook, peel, and slice potatoes. Mix applesauce and cinnamon. In a greased 2-quart baking dish, arrange alternate layers of potato and applesauce, dribbling each layer with honey and fat. Bake, uncovered, in a moderate oven (350°F) 45 minutes, basting occasionally. Serves 6 to 8.

CRANBERRY-GLAZED SWEET POTATOES

6 medium sweet potatoes (3 pounds)
1 cup canned cranberry sauce
½ cup water
¼ cup sugar
½ teaspoon salt
1 teaspoon grated orange rind
½ teaspoon cinnamon
2 tablespoons chicken fat or pareve margarine

Boil, cool, and peel potatoes. Cut each in half lengthwise and place in single layer in a greased baking dish. Combine cranberry sauce, water, sugar, salt, orange rind, and cinnamon. Bring to a boil and simmer 5 minutes. Add fat and stir until melted. Pour cranberry mixture over potatoes and bake in a moderate oven (325°F) 30 minutes or until glazed, basting occasionally. Serves 6.

HONEYED SWEET POTATOES

8 medium sweet potatoes
(4 pounds)
½ cup honey
2 tablespoons grated orange rind
½ cup orange juice
¼ cup chicken fat or pareve margarine
½ teaspoon cinnamon
Dash ginger
¼ teaspoon salt

Cook unpeeled sweet potatoes until tender. Peel; cut into ½-inch slices. Combine honey, orange rind, orange juice, fat, cinnamon, ginger, and salt in a large skillet. Bring to a boil, reduce heat, and simmer 5 minutes. Add potatoes and simmer 5 minutes more, basting frequently with the sauce. Serves 8.

ORANGE-GLAZED SWEET POTATOES

8 medium sweet potatoes
(4 pounds)
12-ounce jar orange marmalade
2 tablespoons chicken fat or vegetable shortening
¼ cup water
¼ teaspoon salt

Boil potatoes until just tender; peel. Cut in half lengthwise or into ¾-inch-thick slices. In a large skillet, mix marmalade, fat, water, and salt. Bring to a boil. Add potatoes and cook over moderate heat, basting and turning frequently, until glazed. Serves 8.

SWEET-POTATO-AND-PRUNE CASSEROLE

6 medium sweet potatoes
(3 pounds)
1-pound jar stewed prunes
(drain and save juice)
¾ cup honey
¾ cup teaspoon cinnamon
1 teaspoon salt
2 tablespoons prune juice
2 tablespoons lemon juice
¼ cup melted pareve margarine or chicken fat

Cook potatoes until tender; skin and cut into ¼-inch-thick slices. Cut prunes in half and remove pits. Combine honey, cinnamon, salt, prune juice, lemon juice, and melted fat. In a 2-quart casserole, arrange alternate layers of sweet potatoes and prunes, pouring some of the honey mixture over each layer. Bake, uncovered, in a moderate oven (350°F) 45 minutes, basting occasionally with the syrup in the baking dish. Serves 6 to 8.

VEGETABLE MEDLEY

10½-ounce can condensed clear chicken soup, undiluted
½ cup liquid from cooked vegetables (see below)
1½ tablespoons potato starch
2 tablespoons chicken fat or pareve margarine
2 cups cooked, sliced carrots
1½ cups (about 16) cooked white onions
cups cooked, chopped spinach

Drain vegetables well and save ½ cup of the liquid. Mix a little of the soup into the potato starch until smooth. Blend in balance of soup and the vegetable liquid. In a greased 1½-quart casserole, arrange alternate layers of vegetables and sauce, with sauce as the top layer. Bake in a moderate oven (375°F) 20 minutes. Serves 6 to 8.

SPRING GARDEN VEGETABLES

¼ cup butter or pareve margarine
1½ pounds summer squash, sliced
1 medium green pepper, diced
1 bunch scallions, sliced
½ cup thin-sliced celery
3 medium tomatoes, peeled and diced
1 teaspoon sugar
1 teaspoon salt
⅛ teaspoon pepper

In a large heavy skillet, sauté squash, pepper, scallions, and celery in the fat until onion is tender. Add tomatoes and seasonings; cook until vegetables are tender. Serves 6.

FRIED BANANAS

1 egg, slightly beaten
1½ teaspoons salt
1 tablespoon water
4 large bananas, firm and green-tipped
½ cup matzo meal
Shortening for frying

Heat shortening, one inch deep, to 375°F in a large skillet. Combine egg, salt, and water. Peel bananas and slice crosswise into pieces 1-inch thick. Dip in egg mixture. Roll in matzo meal. Fry in the hot fat 1½ to 2 minutes or until golden brown and tender. Drain on absorbent paper. Serve hot as a side dish with meat, fish, or poultry. Serves 4 or 5.

VELVET VEGETABLE SAUCE

¼ cup canned condensed clear chicken soup, undiluted
2 teaspoons finely minced onion
1 cup mayonnaise
½ teaspoon lemon juice

Bring the soup and onion to a boil. Remove from heat and add mayonnaise gradually, stirring without stopping. Cook in a double boiler until very thick, stirring continuously. Remove from heat and add lemon juice. Serve on any hot cooked vegetable.

POTATO KUGELACH

2 eggs
2 cups water
¼ cup peanut oil or chicken fat
¼ cup matzo meal
6-ounce package (or two 3-oz.) potato-pancake mix

Beat eggs with fork until blended. Add water and oil or chicken fat. Stir in matzo meal and potato-pancake mix. Allow batter to thicken for 3 minutes. Fill greased muffin pans and bake in a hot oven (450°F) 40 to 45 minutes or until well browned and crusty. Loosen with a knife and remove from pan. Makes 12, which will serve 6 to 8.

EASIEST POTATO KUGEL

2 eggs
2 cups water
¼ cup peanut oil or melted chicken fat
¼ cup matzo meal
6-ounce (or two 3-oz.) package potato-mix

Beat eggs with a fork until blended. Add water and oil or fat; mix well. Stir in matzo meal and potato-pancake mix. Allow batter to thicken for 3 minutes. Spread in a very well-greased 8 × 1¼-inch layer-cake pan. Bake in a hot oven (450°F) one hour or until as brown as desired. Serves 6 to 8.

VEGETABLES AND SIDE DISHES

EASY "GRATED" POTATO KUGEL

6 medium-sized white potatoes (2½ pounds)
1 large onion
1 large carrot
¼ cup matzo meal
1½ teaspoons salt
¼ teaspoon white pepper
2 eggs, beaten
¼ cup peanut oil

Pare vegetables and put through a meat grinder, using the fine blade. Add remaining ingredients and mix thoroughly. Pour into a well-greased 1½-quart baking dish. Bake in a moderate oven (375°F) about one hour or until top is browned and crisp at the edges. Serves 6 to 8.

MATZO-MEAL KUGEL

2 large onions, diced
¾ cup celery, diced
6 tablespoons chicken fat
2½ cups matzo meal
¼ cup minced parsley
1¼ teaspoons salt
⅛ teaspoon pepper
3 eggs, slightly beaten
10½-ounce can condensed clear chicken soup, undiluted
1½ cups water

Sauté onion and celery in fat until tender. Remove from heat. Add matzo meal, parsley, and seasonings. Combine eggs, soup, and water. Add to matzo-meal mixture. Pour into greased 1½-quart baking dish and bake at 375°F one hour or until set and lightly browned. For a crisper kugel, bake in a larger, shallow pan. Serves 6.

MATZO KUGEL*

1 cup minced onion
1 cup finely diced celery
6 tablespoons chicken fat or pareve margarine
6 matzos, broken into small pieces**
1 teaspoon salt
¼ teaspoon pepper
2 teaspoons paprika
2 eggs, slightly beaten
10½-ounce can condensed clear chicken soup, undiluted
1¼ cups hot water

Sauté onions and celery in the fat until onion is tender. Add broken matzos. Combine remaining ingredients and add to matzo mixture. Pour into a well-greased 1½-quart baking dish. Place in a moderate oven (375°F) and bake 30 minutes or until firm. Serves 6 to 8.

*If you prefer a sweet kugel to serve with meat or chicken, look in the chapter entitled "Sweet Things," page 174.

**3½ cups matzo farfel may be used instead.

CRUNCHY STUFFING BALLS

6 matzos, finely broken*
½ cup pareve margarine or chicken fat
½ cup minced onion
½ cup minced celery
¼ teaspoon salt
⅛ teaspoon pepper
1 tablespoon paprika
1 egg, slightly beaten
¼ cup chopped parsley
10½-ounce can condensed clear chicken soup, undiluted
1 cup chopped walnuts

Sauté onion and celery in the fat until tender but not brown. Add broken matzos and toast lightly. Combine salt, pepper, paprika, egg, parsley, and soup. Add nuts and soup mixture to matzo mixture. Shape into 2-inch balls (an easy way is to pack into a ⅓-cup measuring cup) and place on a greased cookie sheet. Bake in a moderate oven (375°F) 20 minutes or until crisp and brown. Serves 6 to 8.

*4 cups matzo farfel may be used instead.

SAVORY MATZO FARFEL

2 large onions, minced
¼ cup chicken fat or pareve margarine
3½ cups matzo farfel
1 teaspoon salt
¼ teaspoon pepper
1 teaspoon paprika
10½-ounce can condensed clear chicken soup, undiluted
1 cup water

Sauté onion in fat until tender, using a large skillet. Add matzo farfel and stir until lightly browned. Combine seasonings, condensed chicken soup, and water. Add slowly to the skillet and cook over low heat, stirring frequently, until all the liquid is absorbed. Serve as a side dish with meat or poultry. Serves 6.

FARFEL RING

1 cup minced onion
1 cup finely diced celery
6 tablespoons chicken fat or pareve margarine
3½ cups matzo farfel
1 teaspoon salt
¼ teaspoon pepper
2 teaspoons paprika
2 eggs, slightly beaten
10½-ounce can condensed clear chicken soup, undiluted
1¼ cups boiling water

Sauté onion and celery in the fat until tender; add matzo farfel. Combine seasonings, eggs, and condensed chicken soup; pour into matzo-farfel mixture. Add boiling water and set aside until all the liquid is absorbed. Pack into a greased ring mold and let sit for about 5 minutes. Turn out on a greased cookie sheet or heatproof platter and bake in a moderate oven (375°F) 30 minutes. Fill center as desired. Serves 6.

BAKED THINGS

BAKED THINGS

Cakes baked from scratch

Don't touch that oven until you read and digest pages 10-12. Baking is simple if a few basic rules are followed. If you take liberties with instructions, you must also accept the responsibility for the results.

Eggs are important in most baking, but for Passover they get special attention because they provide lightness and volume that at other times of the year can be obtained with yeast or other leavening. Did your mother, like mine, order a case of eggs for Pesach? Between the hard-cooked eggs to be served with salt water during the Seders, and the matzo balls and the sponge cakes, they were always used up. Traditional Passover foods are not designed for people on low cholesterol diets.

Use large eggs in all these baking recipes. Extra large or jumbo eggs are fine in other dishes, if you want to use them, but such outsized eggs will change the proportions of baked items. Jewish people tend to be overly generous with food—if a little is good, a lot is better. In this instance, generosity can cause costly and frustrating failures.

Because most Passover cakes require separated eggs, it makes sense to review the method:

1. Use fresh eggs. Eggs that are not refrigerated become stale. As eggs age, the whites get watery and they will not whip up as they should.

2. The better the grade of eggs, the better the results.

3. It is easier to separate eggs when they are cold. Let them reach room temperature before beating.

4. An egg separator makes this task simple, because the yolk is caught in a special indentation, and the white is collected in the cup that is placed underneath.

5. If an egg separator is not available, crack egg gently and pour it back and forth between the two eggshell halves over a cup or small bowl to separate the yolk from the white.

6. Do not add the separated white to the balance of the whites in the mixing bowl until you are sure that the yolk is intact. Egg yolk in egg whites prevents their whipping up properly.

7. Foreign matter of any kind can make it difficult to whip egg whites. Take necessary precautions. Be sure beaters are dry and spotless, without a trace of grease or oil.

8. Beat egg whites at high speed. For most recipes, they are ready if, when the beater is lifted, a peak forms and tips over slightly at the top. Do not overbeat or they will start to break down.

9. Do not allow beaten whites to stand, either at room temperature or in the refrigerator. This causes them to break down and they cannot be beaten again.

10. The most efficient tool for folding egg whites into the batter is a rubber scraper. Cut down through the center of the bowl and fold the batter over the whites. Continue, using a light touch and working all around the bowl until no more free egg white is visible.

Once you put the cake in the oven, don't peek. Every time you open the oven door, you let in cold air. Assuming your oven temperature is accurate, there is no reason to be concerned. If you must reassure yourself, at least wait until about two-thirds of the baking time has elapsed. This gives the cake time to rise and set.

You now have all the information you need to make you an expert Passover cake baker. Zol zein mit glick (lots of luck).

NINE-EGG PASSOVER SPONGE CAKE

9 eggs, separated
2 cups sugar
6 tablespoons water
2½ teaspoons grated lemon rind
¼ cup lemon juice
¾ cup cake meal, unsifted
¾ cup potato starch, unsifted
½ teaspoon salt

Beat egg yolks slightly; gradually beat in sugar until mixture is light and fluffy. Add water, lemon rind, and lemon juice; beat thoroughly. Gradually mix in cake meal and potato starch. Beat egg whites with salt until stiff but not dry. Fold into batter gently but thoroughly. Pour into an ungreased 10-inch tube pan. Bake in a slow oven (325°F) 1¼ hours or until cake springs back when touched lightly. Invert pan and cool thoroughly before removing cake.

SIX-EGG PASSOVER SPONGE CAKE

6 eggs, separated
1⅓ cups sugar
¼ cup water
1½ teaspoons grated lemon rind
3 tablespoons lemon juice
½ cup cake meal, unsifted
½ cup potato starch, unsifted
¼ teaspoon salt

Beat egg yolks slightly; gradually beat in sugar until mixture is light and fluffy. Add water, lemon rind, and lemon juice; beat thoroughly. Gradually mix in cake meal and potato starch. Beat egg whites with salt until stiff but not dry. Fold into batter gently but thoroughly. Pour into an ungreased 9-inch tube pan. Bake in a slow oven (325°F) 1 hour and 10 minutes or until cake springs back when touched lightly with a finger. Invert pan and cool thoroughly before removing cake.

POTATO-STARCH SPONGE CAKE

7 eggs
1½ cups sugar, sifted
1½ tablespoons lemon juice
1½ teaspoons grated lemon rind
¾ cup potato starch, sifted
Dash salt

For a feathery-light and delicate cake, try this one. It is not the traditional Passover sponge-cake texture, but many people prefer it. This cake has an additional advantage for people who cannot use wheat products, because it contains none.

Separate six of the eggs. Beat the six yolks and the one whole egg until frothy. Gradually add sifted sugar, lemon juice, and lemon rind, beating constantly and thoroughly. Then gradually add sifted potato starch, stirring constantly to ensure thorough blending. Beat the egg whites with the salt until stiff but not dry. Fold gently but thoroughly into egg-yolk mixture. Place in ungreased 10-inch tube pan. Bake in a moderate oven (350°F) about 55 minutes or until cake springs back when touched gently with fingers. Invert pan and cool thoroughly before removing cake.

NUT TORTE

6 eggs, separated
1⅓ cups sugar
¼ cup water
1½ teaspoons grated lemon rind
3 tablespoons lemon juice
½ cup cake meal, unsifted
½ cup potato starch, unsifted
¼ teaspoon salt
1 cup chopped walnuts

Beat egg yolks slightly; gradually beat in the sugar until mixture is light and fluffy. Add water, lemon rind, and lemon juice; beat thoroughly. Gradually, mix in cake meal and potato starch. Beat egg whites with salt until stiff but not dry. Fold chopped nuts and beaten egg whites into the batter gently but thoroughly. Pour into an ungreased 9-inch tube pan.* Bake in a moderate oven (325°F) 1¼ hours or until cake springs back when touched lightly. Invert pan and cool thoroughly before removing cake.

*To bake a 10-inch cake, use 9 eggs, 2 cups sugar, 6 tablespoons water, 2½ teaspoons grated lemon rind, ¼ cup lemon juice, ½ teaspoon salt, ¾ cup cake meal, ¾ cup potato starch, 1½ cups chopped walnuts. Use a 10-inch tube pan and bake about 5 minutes extra.

CHIFFON CAKE

1 cup cake meal, unsifted
¼ cup potato starch, unsifted
1½ cups sugar
1 teaspoon salt
½ cup peanut oil
8 eggs, separated
½ cup water
¼ cup lemon juice
1 tablespoon grated lemon rind

Tender and moist, this cake looks like a sponge cake but stays fresh much longer.

Combine cake meal, potato starch, sugar, and salt in a mixing bowl. Make a well in the center; add in order the oil, egg yolks, water, lemon juice, and lemon rind. Beat until very smooth (about 5 minutes at medium speed on an electric mixer). Beat egg whites until very stiff. DO NOT UNDERBEAT. Pour egg-yolk mixture slowly over the whites; gently fold in until just blended. DO NOT STIR. Pour into an ungreased 10-inch tube pan and bake in a moderate oven (325°F) 1 hour and 10 minutes. Invert pan immediately; hang over the neck of a funnel or bottle and cool thoroughly. Cut from pan with a spatula or table knife.

BANANA-NUT CHIFFON CAKE

1 cup cake meal
¼ cup potato starch
1½ cups sugar
1 teaspoon salt
½ cup peanut oil
8 eggs, separated
1 cup mashed ripe banana
2 teaspoons grated lemon rind
¾ cup chopped walnuts

Combine cake meal, potato starch, sugar, and salt in a bowl. Add in order the oil, egg yolks, banana, and lemon rind. Beat until smooth (about 5 minutes at medium speed on an electric mixer). Beat egg whites until very stiff. DO NOT UNDERBEAT. Pour egg-yolk mixture slowly over the whites; gently fold in until just blended. At the same time, fold in chopped nuts. DO NOT STIR. Pour into an ungreased 10-inch tube pan and bake in a moderate oven (325°F) 1 hour and 10 minutes. Invert pan immediately; hang over neck of a funnel or bottle and cool thoroughly. Cut from pan with a spatula or table knife.

CHEESE CAKE

2 cups matzo meal
½ cup granulated sugar
1½ teaspoons cinnamon
½ cup melted butter
4 eggs
1 cup granulated sugar
1½ tablespoons lemon juice
⅛ teaspoon salt
1 cup light cream
3 cups (1½ pounds) cream-style cottage cheese
2 tablespoons potato starch
2 teaspoons grated lemon rind

Cheese cake in any form is sinfully rich. This Passover version uses cottage cheese because it not only produces a delicious cake but also is a little less of a strain on the waistline. You may use your own cream-cheese filling in the crust if you wish, but my conscience would not allow me to tempt you that far.

Combine matzo meal with the next 3 ingredients. Save about ¾ cup of this mixture. Press the rest into the bottom and about 2 inches up the sides of an ungreased 9-inch spring-form pan. Beat eggs until light and fluffy; gradually beat in the 1 cup of sugar. Add the next 5 ingredients and beat until well blended. Sieve entire mixture through a medium strainer. Stir in lemon rind. Pour into the pan. Sprinkle with remaining matzo-meal mixture. Bake in a moderate oven (350°F) one hour. Turn off heat; open oven door slightly; allow to cool in oven at least one hour. Chill thoroughly. Remove side of pan.

REFRIGERATOR LOAF CAKE

½ of a 6-egg sponge cake*
1-pound can cranberry sauce
1 egg white
½ cup sliced almonds
1 cup heavy cream, chilled (optional)
2 tablespoons sugar (optional)

Cut cake into ⅓-inch-thick slices. Mash cranberry sauce until smooth. Beat egg white until stiff; fold in cranberry sauce and nuts. In a loaf pan, place alternate layers of cake and sauce, starting and ending with cake. Cover with waxed paper; place a weight on top; chill for several hours or overnight. Loosen around edges with a knife and unmold onto a serving plate. If desired, frost with whipped cream, made by beating the chilled cream until slightly thickened and then beating in the sugar until thick.

*Made with Passover sponge-cake mix if desired.

APPLE CRUMB CAKE

2½ cups matzo meal
6 tablespoons sugar
1 tablespoon cinnamon
¾ cup melted butter
2 15-ounce jars applesauce
(3½ cups)
¾ cup raisins
½ cup chopped walnuts
Ginger

This recipe is a cake and yet not a cake, because it is not made with the usual ingredients and does not have the usual appearance. This kind of cake is popular in the Scandinavian countries.

Mix matzo meal, sugar, and cinnamon; blend in butter thoroughly. Brown in a moderate oven (350°F) 15 minutes, stirring occasionally. Press ¾ of the crumbs firmly on the bottom and 1½ inches up the sides of a 9-inch spring-form pan. Mix applesauce, raisins, and nuts. Pour into pan and spread evenly. Top with remaining crumb mixture and sprinkle with ginger. Bake in a moderate oven (350°F) one hour. Cool at least one hour before removing side of pan. Serve warm or cold, plain or with cream.

Cookies baked from scratch

While there is no need to apologize for cookies baked from mixes, much can be said for the originality possible when cookies are baked from scratch. True, more ingredients must be measured, more time is needed, and more work is involved. The reward, though, is the knowledge that you are capable of executing all the required steps of a recipe.

Always use a flat baking sheet for cookies, unless otherwise stated in a recipe. Sides on a baking pan prevent adequate heat distribution and browning. The use of special baking paper precludes the need to grease pans and scrub them later. What is creative about that?

FUDGE BROWNIES

3½ ounces bittersweet chocolate
¼ cup butter or pareve margarine
2 eggs
⅛ teaspoon salt
⅔ cup sugar
½ cup cake meal
½ cup coarsely chopped walnuts

Melt chocolate and butter or margarine over hot water. Cool. Beat eggs and salt until thick and lemon-colored. Gradually beat in sugar. Beat in cooled chocolate mixture. Gradually add cake meal and beat until well blended. Stir in chopped nuts. Spread batter evenly in a well-greased 8-inch-square pan. Bake in a moderate oven (350°F) 35 minutes. Cut into 2-inch squares while still hot. Cool in pan. Makes 16.

MOCHA FUDGE BROWNIES

2¾ ounces bittersweet chocolate
¼ cup butter or pareve margarine
2 eggs
⅛ teaspoon salt
⅔ cup sugar
½ cup cake meal
1 tablespoon instant-coffee powder
½ cup coarsely chopped walnuts

Melt chocolate and butter over hot water. Cool. Beat eggs and salt until very thick. Gradually beat in sugar. Beat in cooled chocolate mixture. Mix cake meal with instant coffee. Gradually add cake-meal mixture and beat until well blended. Stir in chopped nuts. Spread batter evenly in a well-greased 8-inch-square pan. Bake in a moderate oven (350°F) 35 minutes. Cut into portions while still hot. Cool in pan. Makes 16.

DATE-NUT KISSES

1½ cups (8 ounces) chopped dates
1½ cups chopped nuts
1½ teaspoons grated lemon rind
2 tablespoons cake meal
2 egg whites
Dash salt
1 cup sugar

Combine dates, nuts, lemon rind, and cake meal. Set aside. Beat egg whites and salt until frothy. Gradually add sugar, about 2 tablespoons at a time, and beat well after each addition. Continue to beat until stiff peak is formed when beater is lifted slowly. Fold in date mixture gently but thoroughly. Line cookie sheets with unglazed paper. (Special baking paper is available in food stores.) Drop by teaspoonsful onto the lined cookie sheets. Bake in a slow oven (250°F) 30 minutes. Remove to cooling racks immediately. Makes 40.

NUT COOKIES

1 cup butter or pareve margarine
4 eggs
1 cup sugar
1 cup cake meal
1½ cups chopped nuts
½ teaspoon salt
2 teaspoons grated lemon rind

Cream butter or margarine until soft. Beat in eggs and sugar until light and fluffy. Stir in cake meal, nuts, salt, and lemon rind. Drop by teaspoonful onto well-greased cookie sheets, at least 2 inches apart, to allow for spreading. Bake in a moderate oven (375°F) 10 minutes or until browned at edges. Makes 4 dozen.

FRUIT-NUT CHEWS

2 cups matzo meal
2 cups matzo farfel
1¼ cups sugar
1 teaspoon cinnamon
¼ teaspoon ginger
1 teaspoon salt
1 cup chopped walnuts
1 cup raisins or chopped dates
3 eggs, well beaten
¾ cup peanut oil
½ cup mashed ripe banana

Combine matzo meal, farfel, sugar, cinnamon, ginger, and salt. Stir in nuts and raisins (or dates). Beat eggs, oil, and banana together very thoroughly. Beat into dry mixture very thoroughly. Drop by teaspoonful onto well-greased cookie sheets. Bake in a moderate oven (350°F) 20 minutes or until browned. Makes about 50.

ALMOND DROP COOKIES

1½ cups whole blanched almonds
2 egg whites
Dash salt
¾ cup sugar

Grind nuts finely in food grinder or blender. Beat egg whites with salt until foamy. Add sugar, 2 tablespoons at a time, beating thoroughly after each addition. Continue to beat until a peak forms when beater is lifted slowly. Fold in ground nuts. Drop by teaspoonful onto well-greased cookie sheets. Bake in a moderate oven (350°F) 15 minutes or until lightly browned. Remove from pans immediately and cool on wire racks. Makes about 3 dozen.

BAKED THINGS

LACY WAFERS

½ cup finely ground blanched almonds
¼ cup sugar
2 teaspoons potato starch
cup melted butter or pareve margarine
1 tablespoon milk or water

Easy does it, since these wafers spread out very thin and lacy. Handle with tender, loving care. The results are worth it.

Use fine blade of food grinder or a blender to grind almonds. Combine them with the remaining ingredients and mix well. Grease cookie sheets generously. Sprinkle with potato starch or cake meal. Drop mixture by half-teaspoonful onto cookie sheets, about 3 inches apart. They will spread! Bake in a moderate oven (350°F) 8 to 10 minutes or until golden brown. Cool on pan about one minute and then remove carefully with a wide spatula to wire racks. Makes about 2 dozen.

Cakes and cookies baked from mixes

The advent of sponge-cake mix in 1952 heralded a major breakthrough in the modernization of Passover baking. Since then, many other cake mixes have been added, making life easier for the homemaker and more festal for her mealtime audiences. Sponge cake can, of course, be baked from scratch, and many women prefer to make their own. However, for those who dislike measuring, this mix is the answer, representing no compromise in texture and flavor. Also, for the small family the mix means that there will be no leftover cake meal and potato starch after the holiday. The one package of mix contains all the dry ingredients plus the flavoring.

Chocolate, honey, and other cakes now made from mixes for Passover cannot be made from scratch. Who ever heard of any homemade Passover cake, except the sponge cake, before mixes appeared? All of this is possible because there are available to manufacturers Kosher for Passover ingredients that cannot be purchased for home use. The personal touch need not disappear, though, even if a mix is used in baking. With a little imagination and the addition of fruits, nuts, spices, and other ingredients, a cake becomes yours alone.

Stretching the imagination a little farther can result in a wide variety of cookies made from cake mixes. Essentially, many drop-cookie recipes are similar to cake recipes. Only the amount of liquid needs to be reduced in these instances to make cookie batter instead of cake batter. The oil that is usually added to the cookie recipes made from cake mixes in this book provides desirable texture and keeping qualities.

BANANA-NUT SPONGE CAKE

12-ounce package Passover sponge-cake mix
¾ cup finely mashed ripe bananas
½ cup chopped nuts
6 eggs, separated

Mix and bake cake as directed on the package, substituting the bananas for the water. While folding in the egg whites, also fold in the nuts.

EASY CHIFFON CAKE

12-ounce package Passover sponge-cake mix
6 eggs, separated
⅓ cup peanut oil
½ cup water

Empty the package of mix into a bowl. Make a well in the center. Add in order the oil, egg yolks, and water. Beat very thoroughly (about 5 minutes at medium speed with an electric mixer). Beat egg whites until very stiff. DO NOT UNDERBEAT. Fold in egg-yolk mixture thoroughly. DO NOT STIR. Pour into an ungreased 9-inch tube pan. Bake in a moderate oven (350°F) one hour. Invert pan immediately; hang over the neck of a funnel or bottle and cool thoroughly. Cut from pan.

EASY COFFEE CHIFFON CAKE

12-ounce package Passover sponge-cake mix
3 tablespoons instant coffee
⅓ cup peanut oil
6 eggs, separated
½ cup water

Empty the package of mix into a bowl; blend in instant coffee. Then mix and bake as directed in Easy Chiffon Cake (page 157).

JELLY ROLL

12-ounce package Passover sponge-cake mix
6 eggs
¼ cup water
Potato starch
Sugar
1 cup (12-ounce jar) raspberry preserves

Line a jelly-roll pan (10½ × 15½ × 1-inch) with waxed paper. Mix batter as directed on sponge-cake-mix package. Bake at 400°F for 20 minutes. Sprinkle a large dish towel with a mixture of half sugar and half potato starch. Turn cake out on towel. Peel off paper carefully. Trim edges of cake if they are hard, but if properly baked, they should not be. Roll up with towel rolled in with the cake. Allow to cool, with the open edge on the bottom, for 10 minutes. Unroll gently, spread with preserves, leaving a one-half-inch border all around. Roll up again, without the towel this time, of course. Wrap in waxed paper and cool on cake rack.

BANANA SPICE CAKE

12-ounce package Passover sponge-cake mix
¾ cup finely mashed bananas
6 eggs, separated
½ teaspoon cinnamon
⅛ teaspoon ginger

Mix and bake cake as directed on box, substituting the bananas for the water and stirring the spices into the box of mix before adding to egg-yolk mixture. Frost as desired and garnish with chopped nuts.

ROZINKES MIT MANDLEN CAKE

Mix batter for one 12-ounce package of Passover coffee-cake mix as directed on the package. Fold in ⅓ cup chopped nuts and ⅓ cup raisins. Spread in pan as directed on package. Add contents of topping packet and bake as usual.

NUT POUND CAKE

Make batter as directed on a 10-ounce package of Passover pound-cake mix. Fold in ½ cup chopped walnuts before placing batter in pan. Bake as usual.

COFFEE POUND CAKE

Mix 3 tablespoons instant coffee into a 10-ounce package of Passover pound-cake mix. Then mix and bake batter as directed on package.

EASY NUT CAKE

Prepare a 12-ounce package of Passover sponge-cake mix as directed on the box. Fold ¾ to 1 cup of chopped walnuts into the batter along with the beaten egg whites.

SPONGE LAYERS

For each 12-ounce package of Passover sponge-cake mix, use either two 9-inch or three 8-inch cake pans. Bake in moderate oven (350°F) 35 minutes. When baking layers, grease and line bottoms of cake pans with waxed paper. To cool, invert pans; do not remove cake until pan is cool to touch. Frost as desired. For strawberry shortcake, fill and top with sweetened whipped cream and sliced strawberries.

SPONGE CUPCAKES

Fill pans ⅔ full and bake at 350°F 25 minutes or until golden brown. Pans may be ungreased and unlined or lined with paper baking cups.

One 12-ounce package of Passover sponge-cake mix makes 30 to 32 medium-size cupcakes.

COFFEE SPONGE CAKE

12-ounce package Passover sponge-cake mix
3 tablespoons instant coffee
6 eggs
¼ cup water

Stir instant coffee thoroughly into box of mix. Combine and bake cake as directed on box. Frost with Coffee Whipped Cream if desired.

COFFEE WHIPPED CREAM

1 cup heavy sweet cream, cold
1½ teaspoons instant coffee
2 tablespoons sugar

Place instant coffee and cold sweet cream in a chilled bowl and whip until it starts to thicken. Add granulated sugar gradually and beat until just thick enough to hold its shape. Spread on top and sides of Coffee Sponge Cake or other cakes.

MOCHA SPONGE CAKE

12-ounce package Passover sponge-cake mix
2 tablespoons instant coffee
6 eggs, separated
¼ cup water
1½ ounces bittersweet chocolate, grated

Stir instant coffee into package of mix. Combine ingredients and bake as directed on box. While folding in beaten egg whites, add the grated chocolate. Frost, if desired, with Coffee Fluff.

COFFEE FLUFF

1 tablespoon instant coffee
5 tablespoons water
2 egg whites, unbeaten
1½ cups brown sugar
Dash salt

Dissolve instant coffee in the water. Place all ingredients in top of double boiler over rapidly boiling water. Beat constantly with hand or electric beater until frosting stands in a peak on beater. Spread on cake. Garnish with walnut halves.

TOASTED ALMOND SPONGE CAKE

12-ounce package Passover sponge-cake mix
6 eggs
¼ cup water
1 cup toasted, slivered almonds

To prepare almonds, place the shelled nuts in a small saucepan, cover with cold water, and bring to a boil. Drain. Slip off skins by pressing between thumb and forefinger. Sliver with a sharp knife while warm. Place in a shallow pan in a slow oven (250°F) about 15 minutes, stirring occasionally until lightly browned.

Prepare cake batter according to directions on the box, folding in ⅔ of the nuts at the same time as the egg whites. Sprinkle remaining ⅓ on the top and bake as directed on box.

SPICE-NUT SPONGE CAKE

12-ounce package Passover sponge-cake mix
2 teaspoons cinnamon
¼ teaspoon ginger
¼ cup Concord-grape wine
6 eggs
½ cup coarsely chopped walnuts

Mix spices into box of mix. Combine and bake cake as directed on box, adding chopped nuts when folding in beaten egg whites.

GOLDEN SPONGE TORTE

12-ounce package Passover sponge-cake mix
6 eggs, separated
¼ cup water
1 cup grated carrots
½ cup chopped walnuts

Combine the sponge-cake mix, egg yolks, and water according to the directions on the package. Fold in the grated carrots and chopped nuts. Then fold in the beaten egg whites. Bake and cool as directed on the package. If desired, frost with whipped cream and decorate with nuts.

CINNAMON-RAISIN SPONGE CAKE

12-ounce package Passover sponge-cake mix
1 tablespoon cinnamon
¼ cup water
6 eggs, separated
1 cup raisins

Stir cinnamon into package of mix. Mix cake as directed on box. While folding in beaten egg whites, add the raisins. Bake as directed on box.

CHOCOLATE-DOT SPONGE CAKE

12-ounce package Passover sponge-cake mix
6 eggs
¼ cup water
2¾ ounces bittersweet chocolate, grated

Combine and bake cake according to the directions on the box. Grated chocolate should be folded into the batter at the same time as the beaten egg whites. Serve plain or frosted with Coffee Whipped Cream (page 160) and decorated with shaved chocolate.

HERMITS

Remember those old-fashioned spicy cookies crammed full of nuts and raisins? Here's a quick and easy version destined for a permanent place in your repertoire.

12-ounce package Passover honey-cake mix
1 tablespoon instant coffee
1 large egg
2 tablespoons peanut oil
Water
1 cup chopped walnuts
1 cup raisins

Stir the coffee into the cake mix. Break the egg into a measuring cup; add the oil; add water to measure a total of ½ cup. Mix as directed on the package. Fold in the raisins and nuts. Chill in refrigerator at least one hour. Drop by teaspoonful onto greased cookie sheets. Bake in a moderate oven (350°F) 15 minutes. They will still be soft. Cool on the cookie sheets one minute and then remove to cooling racks. Makes about 3 dozen.

BANANA-NUT COOKIES

12-ounce package Passover sponge-cake mix
4 eggs, separated
¾ cup mashed bananas
¼ cup peanut oil
½ cup chopped nuts

Allow separated eggs to reach room temperature. Beat yolks with mashed banana and peanut oil until light and fluffy. Add sponge-cake mix gradually and beat very thoroughly. Beat egg whites until stiff. Fold egg whites and chopped nuts into batter gently but thoroughly. Drop by teaspoonful onto well-greased cookie sheets, 2 inches apart. Bake in a moderate oven (375°F) 10 to 12 minutes or until golden brown. Makes about 7 dozen.

NUT DROP COOKIES

12-ounce package Passover sponge-cake mix
4 eggs, separated
¼ cup water
¼ cup peanut oil
¾ cup chopped nuts

Allow separated eggs to reach room temperature. Beat yolks with water and peanut oil until light and fluffy. Add sponge-cake mix gradually and beat very thoroughly. Beat egg whites until very stiff. Fold egg whites and chopped nuts into batter carefully and thoroughly. Drop by teaspoonful onto well-greased cookie sheets and bake in moderate oven (375°F) 10 to 12 minutes or until golden brown. Makes about 4 dozen.

CHOCOLATE NUT CRISPS

12-ounce package Passover chocolate-cake mix
1 large egg
2 tablespoons peanut oil
1 tablespoon water
½ cup chopped nuts

In a large bowl, combine the mix, egg, oil, and water. Beat at medium speed on an electric mixer for 4 minutes. Fold in the nuts. Drop by rounded teaspoonful onto greased cookie sheets, 2 inches apart. Bake at 375°F for 15 minutes. Makes 3½ dozen.

CRUNCHY NUT COOKIES

12-ounce package Passover coffee-cake mix
1 large egg
2 tablespoons peanut oil
1 tablespoon water
½ cup nuts

Empty contents of the large bag into a mixing bowl. Add the egg, oil, and water; mix batter as directed in point 5 on back of box. Fold in nuts and the contents of the small bag. Using measuring teaspoon, drop onto well-greased cookie sheets, 3 inches apart. Bake at 375°F for 12 to 15 minutes or until lightly browned. Makes 3½ dozen.

EASY NUT COOKIES

10-ounce package Passover pound-cake mix
1 large egg
2 tablespoons peanut oil
1 tablespoon water
½ cup chopped nuts

Empty mix into a bowl; add egg, oil, and water. Mix batter as directed in point 5 on back of box. Fold in nuts. Using measuring teaspoon, drop onto well-greased cookie sheets, 3 inches apart. Bake at 375°F for 12 to 15 minutes or until lightly browned. Makes 3½ dozen.

BULL'S-EYE COOKIES

12-ounce box Passover marble-cake mix
1 large egg
2 tablespoons peanut oil
1 tablespoon water
¼ cup chopped nuts

Empty the contents of the large bag into a mixing bowl. Add the egg, oil, and water. Mix batter as directed in points 5 and 6 on back of box. Fold ½ cup chopped nuts into white batter. On greased cookie sheets, using measuring spoons, drop white batter by slightly rounded teaspoonful, 3 inches apart. Top each with a level ½ teaspoonful of chocolate batter. Bake at 350°F for 12 to 15 minutes. Makes 2½ dozen.

HONEY NUT DROPS

12-ounce package Passover honey-cake mix
1 large egg
2 tablespoons peanut oil
Water
½ cup chopped nuts

Break egg into a measuring cup; add the oil; add water to egg and oil to measure a total of ½ cup. Empty cake mix into mixing bowl; add liquid and mix as directed in point 5 on back of box. Fold in nuts. Using measuring teaspoon, drop onto well-greased cookie sheets, 3 inches apart. Bake at 350°F for 15 minutes. They will still be soft. Allow to cool on cookie sheets for one minute before removing to cooling racks. Makes 3½ dozen.

FROSTED WALNUT CRISPS

12-ounce package Passover yellow-cake mix
1 large egg
2 tablespoons peanut oil
1 tablespoon water
½ cup chopped walnuts

Empty the contents of the large bag into a mixing bowl. Add the egg, oil, and water; mix as directed in point 5 on back of box. Fold in nuts. Using measuring teaspoon, drop onto well-greased cookie sheets, 3 inches apart. Bake at 350°F for 12 to 15 minutes or until lightly browned. Make frosting as directed on package. After cookies are thoroughly cooled, top each with a small amount of the frosting. Makes about 3½ dozen.

Pastries

It is not possible to make a tender, flaky, rolled pie crust for Passover, so why bother? A crumb crust is so simple to do and requires no major compromise in texture or flavor. The matzo-meal crust is suggested for all pies and tarts in this book not only because it is crunchy and delicious but also because the ingredients are readily available and modestly priced. For a more lavish crust, use Passover cookie crumbs mixed with melted butter or pareve margarine.

A crumb crust is always baked, cooled, and then filled. Do not try to bake a standard fruit pie in this crust or it will disintegrate.

STRAWBERRY-CREAM TARTS

It's almost impossible to eat only one of these tarts, so bake at your own risk unless you have an iron will or are not concerned about calories.

SHELLS
1½ cups matzo meal
⅔ cup melted butter
3 tablespoons sugar
¼ teaspoon salt
1½ teaspoons cinnamon

FILLING
¼ cup potato starch
1½ cups sugar
3 eggs
1 pint commercial sour cream
¼ teaspoon salt
1 tablespoon butter
6 tablespoons lemon juice
1 cup (approximately) sliced, sugared strawberries

Combine matzo meal with melted butter, sugar, salt, and cinnamon. Place paper baking cups in medium-size muffin pan. Press heaping tablespoon of this mixture into bottom and sides of each baking cup. Bake in a moderate oven (375°F) for 15 to 18 minutes or until well browned. Cool thoroughly in pan before removing.

Combine potato starch and sugar. Beat eggs and sour cream together. Combine both mixtures in top of double boiler. Add salt and butter. Cook, stirring constantly, over boiling water, until thickened (about 5 minutes). Then cook about 15 minutes longer, until very thick, stirring occasionally. Cool; add lemon juice and mix well. Spoon a little of this mixture into each tart shell. Place layer of strawberries on top. Add remaining filling and decorate as desired. Makes 15.

PETITE JAM TARTS

If baking something different appeals to you, then the time and patience needed to make these tarts won't bother you at all. They are worth the effort.

½ pound (1 cup) sweet butter
6 ounces cream cheese
2 eggs, beaten
2 cups cake meal
1¼ cups (approximately) raspberry preserves

Soften butter and cream cheese at room temperature. Combine and beat until smooth and creamy. Beat in eggs. Add cake meal, ½ cup at a time, blending well after each addition. Work with fingers until dough is smooth. Wrap in waxed paper and chill several hours in the refrigerator. Shape into 1-inch balls and place on ungreased baking sheets. With thumb, make a deep well in each, so that bottoms and sides of tarts are ⅛-inch thick. Bake at 425°F for 15 minutes or until golden brown. Cool. Fill wells with preserves. Makes 4 dozen.

BAKED THINGS

CRUNCHY CREAM-CHEESE TARTS

SHELLS

1 cup matzo meal
6 tablespoons melted butter
2 tablespoons sugar
⅛ teaspoon salt
1 teaspoon cinnamon

FILLING

3 eggs
½ cup sugar
⅓ cup lemon juice
1 teaspoon grated lemon rind
8 ounces cream cheese

Combine these five ingredients thoroughly. Place paper baking cups in medium-size muffin pan. Press a heaping tablespoon of this mixture into the bottom and sides of each paper cup. Bake in a moderate oven (375°F) for 15 to 18 minutes or until well browned. Cool thoroughly in pan before removing; then fill. Makes 10.

In the top of a double boiler, beat the eggs until thick. Gradually beat in the sugar, lemon juice, and lemon rind. Cook over boiling water, stirring constantly, until thick and smooth. Cool. Beat this mixture into softened cream cheese until well blended.

MATZO-MEAL PIE CRUST

1 cup matzo meal
2 tablespoons sugar
⅛ teaspoon salt
¼ teaspoon cinnamon
½ cup melted butter or pareve margarine

Blend ingredients well. Press into a 9-inch pie pan and bake in a 375°F oven for 15 to 20 minutes or until golden brown. Cool before filling.

MOCHA CREAM PIE

This pie is spectacular to the eye, ambrosial to the tongue, and gratifying to the soul. I am tempted to say, "Serve for special occasions," but then, what occasion is more special than a family meal?

1 Matzo-Meal Pie Crust
4 teaspoons instant coffee
½ cup boiling water
2½ cups milk
¼ cup potato starch
⅔ cup sugar
⅛ teaspoon salt
3½ ounces bittersweet chocolate, chopped

Combine instant coffee with boiling water and add milk. Mix potato starch, sugar, and salt in the top of a double boiler. Gradually stir in the milk mixture. Add the chopped chocolate. Place over boiling water and stir until blended, about 3 to 5 minutes. Cover and cook 10 minutes longer, stirring occasionally. Cool and pour into the crust. Spread with Coffee Whipped Cream (page 160) and decorate with shaved bittersweet chocolate.

DATE-CHEESE PIE

This is just as tempting as the Cheese Cake (page 151) but smaller in size. I threw in a few dates because I like them.

1 Matzo-Meal Pie Crust (page 167), increasing cinnamon to 1 teaspoon
3 eggs
2 cups (1 pound) cream-style cottage cheese
⅓ cup light sweet cream
⅓ cup sugar
¼ teaspoon salt
1 tablespoon potato starch
1 tablespoon lemon juice
½ cup chopped dates
1½ teaspoons grated lemon rind
3 tablespoons blanched, slivered almonds

Beat eggs until light and fluffy. Gradually beat in the cottage cheese, sweet cream, sugar, salt, potato starch, and lemon juice until well blended. Sieve mixture through a medium strainer. Beat until smooth. Stir in chopped dates and lemon rind. Pour into cooled pie shell. Sprinkle with slivered almonds. Bake in a moderate oven (350°F) 40 minutes or until firm in center. Turn off heat; open oven door slightly and allow to cool in oven for one hour. Chill thoroughly before serving.

LEMON MERINGUE PIE

In this recipe, be sure to bring the meringue out to the very edge of the pie and seal it to the crust. Otherwise it will shrink and look unappetizing.

1 Matzo-Meal Pie Crust (page 167)
5 tablespoons potato starch
¼ teaspoon salt
1 cup sugar
2 cups water
3 eggs, separated
2 tablespoons butter, vegetable shortening, or pareve margarine
5 tablespoons lemon juice
1 tablespoon grated lemon rind
Dash salt
6 tablespoons sugar

Combine potato starch, salt, and ½ cup of the sugar in top of double boiler; add the water. Cook over boiling water until thick, stirring constantly. Cover and cook 10 minutes, stirring occasionally. Combine egg yolks with other ½ cup of sugar. Stir in a little of the hot, cooked mixture rapidly until smooth and pour back. Cook 2 minutes, stirring constantly. Remove from heat. Stir in butter, lemon juice, and rind. Cool to room temperature without stirring (not in the refrigerator). Pour into baked shell. Cover with meringue made by beating the egg whites with the salt until foamy and then gradually beating in the 6 tablespoons sugar. Beat until smooth and glossy. Bake in a moderate oven (325°F) 15 minutes or until lightly browned. Chill and serve.

STRAWBERRIES-AND-CREAM PIE

1 Matzo-Meal Pie Crust (page 167)
¼ cup potato starch
1½ cups sugar
3 eggs
1 pint sour cream
¼ teaspoon salt
1 tablespoon butter
6 tablespoons lemon juice
1 to 1½ cups lightly sugared sliced strawberries

Combine potato starch and sugar. Beat eggs and sour cream together. Combine both mixtures in the top of a double boiler. Add salt and butter. Cook, stirring constantly, over boiling water, until thickened (about 5 minutes). Then cook about 15 minutes longer, until very thick, stirring occasionally. Cool; add lemon juice and mix thoroughly. Pour half this mixture into the cooled crust. Arrange strawberries over this, saving a few to decorate top. Add remaining filling and decorate as desired.

COFFEE-BANANA CREAM PIE

1 Matzo-Meal Pie Crust (page 167)
2 tablespoons instant coffee
2½ cups milk
¼ cup potato starch
⅔ cup sugar
⅛ teaspoon salt
1 tablespoon butter
3 ripe bananas
Sweetened whipped cream

Mix instant coffee and milk. In the top of a double boiler, combine potato starch, sugar, and salt. Gradually add the milk mixture, stirring until smooth. Place over boiling water and stir constantly for 3 minutes or until thickened. Cover and cook 10 minutes more, stirring frequently. Stir in butter. Cool. Place a layer of the filling in the bottom of the pie crust. Slice the bananas and place on top of filling. Add remaining filling. Top with sweetened whipped cream.

PEACH OF A LEMON PIE

1 Matzo-Meal Pie Crust (page 167), increasing cinnamon to 1 teaspoon and adding
½ teaspoon ginger
6 tablespoons potato starch
¼ teaspoon salt
1 cup sugar
2 cups water
3 egg yolks
2 tablespoons butter or pareve margarine
5 tablespoons lemon juice
1 tablespoon grated lemon rind
1¼ cups canned sliced peaches, drained

Combine potato starch, salt, and ½ cup of the sugar in top of double boiler; add the water. Cook over boiling water until thick, stirring constantly. Cover and cook 10 minutes, stirring occasionally. Combine egg yolks with remaining ½ cup sugar. Spoon in a little of the hot cooked mixture. Stir rapidly until smooth and pour back. Cook 2 minutes, stirring constantly. Remove from heat. Stir in butter or margarine, lemon juice, and rind. Cool to room temperature without stirring (not in the refrigerator). Arrange the sliced peaches in the cooled pie crust, saving a few to decorate top. Spread filling over peaches. Garnish with peach slices. Chill and serve.

YOM TOV PRUNE PIE

1 Matzo-Meal Pie Crust (page 167), increasing cinnamon to 1 teaspoon
¾ cup sugar
1 cup chopped dried prunes
2 cups water
3 tablespoons butter or pareve margarine
1½ tablespoons potato starch
3 eggs
2 tablespoons grated lemon rind
6 tablespoons lemon juice
2 teaspoons cinnamon
½ teaspoon ginger
1 cup chopped nuts

Combine sugar, prunes, and water in a saucepan. Simmer over low heat for 10 minutes; add butter or margarine. Mix potato starch with a little of the liquid until smooth; pour back into saucepan. Cook and stir over low heat until mixture comes to a boil. Remove from heat. Beat eggs with lemon rind, lemon juice, cinnamon, ginger, and nuts. Stir a little of the prune mixture into egg mixture. Combine mixtures and cook, stirring constantly, for 5 minutes. Pour into pie shell. Chill thoroughly before serving.

PUFF SHELLS

Equally suitable as a shell for dessert fillings, dinner appetizers, or luncheon main dishes. Note two precautions and your puffs will do you proud. Beat eggs in very thoroughly, the more the better. Secondly, do not open the oven door at all during the early part of the baking and avoid doing so if at all possible until they are done. Other baked items might survive with relatively minor effects, but Puff Shells will be ruined.

1 cup boiling water
⅓ cup peanut oil
½ teaspoon salt
2 teaspoons sugar
1 cup cake meal
4 eggs

In a saucepan, combine the boiling water, oil, salt, and sugar and bring to a slow boil. Reduce heat; add cake meal all at once. Stir vigorously over low heat until mixture forms a ball and leaves the sides of the pan. Remove from heat. Add unbeaten eggs one at a time, beating very thoroughly after each addition until dough is smooth and thick. Drop by heaping tablespoonsful onto well-greased cookie sheet, about 2 inches apart. Bake in a hot oven (400°F) about 40 minutes or until puffed and golden brown. Do not open oven door during early part of baking. Cool, cut off tops, remove excess doughy portions, and put back in oven to dry out, if desired. Fill with sautéed chicken livers, sweetbreads, fruit and whipped cream, or your favorite filling; replace tops. Makes 8.

Bread substitutes

The skeptics who have made dire predictions about the fate of Passover regulations in the hands of the "younger generation" will be reinforced when they see the word "Bread" in a Passover cookbook. They knew it all the time! However, the creative and imaginative homemaker will say, "Why not, as long as no chometzdige ingredients are used?"

Of course the recipes that follow are not breads in the ordinary sense of the word. They are only substitutes that are welcome to enhance meal planning, especially for the lunch-box set.

PASSOVER MUFFINS

¾ cup matzo meal
½ cup cake meal
¾ teaspoon salt
2 tablespoons sugar
4 eggs, separated
¾ cup milk
2 tablespoons melted butter

Mix matzo meal, cake meal, salt, and sugar. Beat egg yolks slightly; add milk and cooled butter; beat thoroughly. Add dry ingredients and mix until well blended. Beat egg whites until stiff but not dry. Fold into batter until no more free egg white is visible. Divide evenly in a greased, 12-muffin tin, medium size. Bake in a moderate oven (350°F) 35 minutes or until golden brown. Makes 12.

TZIBELLE MATZO*

Cut an onion in half. Rub matzos with the cut side of the onion. Brush with melted butter (or for a meat meal, with melted chicken fat) and sprinkle with salt. Brown in a hot oven (425°F) for 3 to 5 minutes.

*This is a very old favorite recipe. For a modern version, mix a little onion powder or garlic powder with the butter, chicken fat, or pareve margarine.

PASSOVER ROLLS

2 cups matzo meal
1 teaspoon salt
1 tablespoon sugar
1 cup water
½ cup peanut oil
4 eggs

More like a French brioche or a hearty cream-puff shell, these rolls are the ideal carrier for fillings. They are so neat when lunch must be taken to school or work.

Combine matzo meal with salt and sugar. Bring oil and water to a boil. Add to matzo-meal mixture and mix well. Beat in eggs thoroughly, one at a time. Allow to stand 15 minutes. With oiled hands, shape into rolls and place on a well-greased cookie sheet. Bake in a moderate oven (375°F) 50 minutes or until golden brown. Makes 12.

PASSOVER BAGEL

½ cup peanut oil
1 cup water
1 teaspoon salt
1 tablespoon sugar
2 cups matzo meal
4 eggs
1 egg, slightly beaten (optional)

Like the ones you buy hot on Sunday morning all year, they are not. But for Passover, they are a delicious change with breakfast or lunch.

Bring oil, water, salt, and sugar to a boil. Add matzo meal and mix well. Beat in 4 eggs thoroughly, one at a time. Allow to stand 15 minutes. Divide dough into 12 pieces, the size of a large egg. With oiled hands, roll each one into a 6-inch rope and shape into a circle. Place on a well-greased baking sheet; brush with beaten egg if desired. Bake in moderate oven (375°F) for 50 minutes or until golden brown. Makes 12.

SWEET THINGS

SWEET THINGS

Something sweet to end a meal, which is not cake, cookies, or pastry, will be found here. What is kugel or kigel to many Jews is shalet or charlotte to Jews from the Bavarian area, or pudding to Yankees. Just don't call it pudying, please.

But "sweet things" serve other purposes than dessert. During the years of the Great Depression, ten cents for the movies bought two feature films, at least one serial, and many cartoons—average sitting time, four or five hours. Oh, yes, for the same ten cents each child got a comic book and an ice cream.

What Jewish mother would let her child sit so long without something to eat? He could fade away to nothing and never be heard from again. All year it was no big problem, because candy, popcorn, and soda, besides the ice cream, could control the emergency. But Pesach presented a problem with only one solution. A CARE package had to be prepared. In those days, before delicious Passover candies were sold, Jewish mothers made various sweets at home.

One solution was to stuff pitted prunes with almonds and then cook them in honey until well glazed. Sticky but fabulous. However, the sticky prunes, wrapped in brown paper (few people trusted the Kashruth of waxed paper in those days), got all over everything else in the brown-paper bag and eventually dripped through, turning the child carrying it into a walking fly trap.

The confections in this section will create no such problem.

DESSERT WINE SAUCE

¼ cup sugar
2 tablespoons potato starch
¼ teaspoon salt
½ cup water
1 cup Concord-grape wine
1 teaspoon lemon juice
1 cup fruit cocktail, drained

Combine first three ingredients in a small saucepan. Gradually blend in the water. Cook over moderate heat until thick, stirring constantly. Gradually blend in the wine and lemon juice; cook about 2 minutes longer or until thickened again. Cool. Add drained fruit cocktail. Spoon over sponge-cake wedges or ice cream.

GOURMET PARFAIT

3 cups sponge cake,* cut into ½-inch cubes
¼ cup sweet wine
1 cup fruit cocktail, drained
1 cup cream, whipped**

In parfait or sherbet glasses, arrange alternate layers of cake cubes, fruit cocktail, and whipped cream, sprinkling each cake layer generously with the wine. Chill and serve. Serves 6.

*May be made with Passover sponge-cake mix.

**The secret of perfect whipped cream is ice-cold cream, bowl, and beater. Beat just until the cream holds its shape. Overbeat and you'll have butter.

LEMON MERINGUE CHARLOTTE

2 matzos, broken*
2 cups milk, scalded
3 tablespoons lemon juice
1 tablespoon grated lemon rind
3 tablespoons melted butter
2 egg yolks and 1 whole egg
¼ teaspoon salt
¼ cup sugar
¼ cup raspberry preserves
2 egg whites
¼ cup sugar

Pour scalded milk over broken matzos and let stand about 15 minutes. Beat well with egg beater or electric mixer. Add lemon juice and rind, butter, eggs, salt, and ¼ cup sugar. Mix well. Pour into greased 1½-quart baking dish, set dish in a pan of hot water, and bake 30 minutes in a slow (300°F) oven. Spread top with preserves. Cover with meringue made by beating egg whites until stiff but not dry and gradually beating in the sugar until the mixture is smooth and glossy. Return to oven to brown meringue, about 15 minutes. Chill before serving. Serves 6.

*1¼ cups matzo farfel may be used instead.

PEACH SHALET

6 matzos,* broken into small pieces
¾ cup chopped nuts
6 tablespoons melted butter or pareve margarine
1 cup juice from canned peaches
¼ cup lemon juice
2 eggs, beaten
1 large can sliced cling peaches, drained
½ cup sugar
1½ teaspoons cinnamon
¾ teaspoon ginger

Combine matzos, nuts, butter, peach juice, lemon juice, and eggs. Combine peaches, sugar, and spices. Place alternate layers of matzo mixture and peach mixture in a greased 1½-quart baking dish. Bake in a moderate oven (375°F) about 40 minutes or until firm and brown. Serve plain or with whipped cream.

*4 cups matzo farfel may be used instead.

MOCHA PUDDING

4 teaspoons instant coffee
½ cup boiling water
2½ cups milk
¼ cup potato starch
⅔ cup sugar
⅛ teaspoon salt
3½ ounces bittersweet chocolate, chopped

Combine instant coffee with the boiling water; add the milk. Mix potato starch, sugar, and salt in the top of a double boiler. Gradually stir in milk mixture. Add chopped chocolate. Place over boiling water and stir until blended, about 3 minutes. Cover and cook 10 minutes longer, stirring occasionally. Pour into sherbet glasses. Cool. Serves 4 to 6.

FRUIT MERINGUE CHARLOTTE

1½ cups matzo farfel*
2 cups prune juice**
1 tablespoon lemon juice
2 teaspoons grated lemon rind
3 tablespoons melted vegetable shortening (or butter for a dairy meal)
2 egg yolks and 1 whole egg
¼ teaspoon salt
¼ cup sugar
½ cup chopped nuts
1½ cups sliced banana or apple
2 egg whites
¼ cup sugar

Pour prune juice over matzo farfel and allow to stand at least 15 minutes. Add next 7 ingredients, beating thoroughly. Pour into greased 1½-quart baking dish. Arrange sliced fruit on top. Bake in a moderate oven (350°F) 25 minutes or until set. Cover pudding with a meringue made by beating egg whites until foamy and then gradually beating in the remaining ¼ cup of sugar until mixture is smooth, glossy, and forms a firm peak. Return to oven to brown meringue, about 15 minutes. Best when served warm. Serves 6 to 8.

*2½ matzos, finely broken, may be used instead.

**Apple juice may be used instead.

CREAMY MOCHA SHALET

3½ ounces bittersweet chocolate
2½ cups milk
¾ cup sugar
2 tablespoons instant coffee
¼ teaspoon salt
1½ cups matzo farfel
1 egg, slightly beaten
3 tablespoons butter
½ cup chopped walnuts

Melt chocolate in top of double boiler. Add 2 cups of the milk and the sugar, coffee, salt, and farfel. Cook over hot water, stirring frequently, about 10 minutes or until thickened. Mix egg with remaining ½ cup milk. Add to hot mixture. Stir well. Add butter and nuts. Continue cooking until butter melts and mixture is again thickened. Pour into 6 to 8 individual serving dishes. Chill. Top with whipped cream and garnish with shaved chocolate or chopped nuts.

BANANA-NUT KUGEL

3 cups matzo farfel
4 eggs
½ teaspoon salt
6 tablespoons sugar
¼ cup melted butter or pareve margarine
2 medium, unripe bananas, sliced
½ cup chopped nuts

Pour cold water over farfel and drain immediately so that farfel is moist but not soggy. Beat eggs with salt, sugar, and melted fat. Mix with farfel. In a greased 1½-quart baking dish, place half the farfel mixture. Arrange the sliced bananas on top and sprinkle with the nuts. Top with the balance of the farfel mixture. Bake in a moderate oven (350°F) 45 minutes or until set and lightly browned. Serves 6.

APPLE MATZO KUGEL

4 matzos
3 eggs, well beaten
½ teaspoon salt
½ cup sugar
¼ cup melted butter, chicken fat, or pareve margarine
1 teaspoon cinnamon
½ cup chopped walnuts
2 large apples, pared and chopped
½ cup raisins
Butter, chicken fat, or pareve margarine

This recipe almost had a nervous breakdown because its place in the book was changed so many times. You find it here because it is a sweet thing and makes a grand dessert. You Litvaks and others who like sweet kugel as a side dish with meat, "Geh gesunterheit und ess gesunterheit" (by all means do as you like). What could be bad?

Break matzos into pieces. Soak in water until soft. Drain but do not squeeze dry. Beat eggs with salt, sugar, melted fat, and cinnamon. Add to matzo mixture. Stir in chopped nuts, chopped apples, and raisins. Dot with additional fat. Bake in a moderate oven (350°F) 45 minutes or until lightly browned. Serves 6.

APPLE-CRUMB PUDDING

Good sponge cake is never left over, so hide a piece to use in this recipe.

6 (2 pounds) eating apples, peeled, cored, and sliced thin
2 tablespoons lemon juice
⅓ cup sugar
¾ teaspoon cinnamon
⅛ teaspoon ginger
4 cups sponge cake,* cut into small cubes
½ cup (1 stick) butter or pareve margarine, melted

Mix apple slices with lemon juice, sugar, cinnamon, and ginger. Toss cake cubes with melted fat. Place ⅓ of the cake crumbs in a greased 12×7½×1¾-inch baking dish. Top with half the apple mixture. Repeat. Spread remaining cake crumbs on top. Cover (use aluminum foil if pan has no cover) and bake in a moderate oven (375°F) 30 minutes. Uncover and bake 30 minutes more or until apples are tender. For a dairy meal, serve with whipped cream if desired. Serves 6 to 8.

*May be made with Passover sponge-cake mix.

SWEET THINGS

CRUNCHY APPLE-ORANGE MEICHEL

3 cups applesauce
2 tablespoons orange juice
¼ teaspoon ginger
1 teaspoon cinnamon
3 tablespoons melted butter
1½ teaspoons grated orange rind
½ cup matzo meal
½ cup sugar

Combine first 4 ingredients. Place in 6 custard cups. Combine last 4 ingredients. Sprinkle this crumb mixture on top of mixture in custard cups. Bake in a hot oven (425°F) 20 minutes. Serves 6.

PEARS CONCORD

1 large can Bartlett pears*
½ cup Concord-grape wine

Drain pears. Boil syrup until concentrated to ½ cup. Add wine to syrup. Stir well and pour over drained pears. Chill thoroughly and serve. Serves 6.

*Elberta peaches, cling peaches, or fruit cocktail may be used instead of pears.

SPICY FRUIT SAUCE

1½ cups dried apricots
2 tablespoons lemon juice
1-pound, 9-ounce jar applesauce
¾ cup raisins
1 teaspoon cinnamon
¼ teaspoon ginger
3 tablespoons sugar

Place apricots and lemon juice in a saucepan; add water until fruit is just covered. Do not cover pan. Simmer 30 minutes or until very tender. Beat until mashed. Add applesauce, raisins, cinnamon, ginger, and sugar. Mix well and cook over low heat for a few minutes. Serve hot or cold. Serves 6.

FRUIT MERINGUES

Don't tell anyone how easy this was to do; they'll think you worked half the day on this meichel.

3 egg whites
Pinch salt
¾ cup sugar
1 tablespoon lemon juice
1 teaspoon grated lemon rind
6 canned peach or pear halves
6 teaspoons raspberry preserves
¼ cup chopped walnuts

Beat egg whites with salt until foamy. Add sugar very gradually, beating well after each addition. Add lemon juice and rind with the last of the sugar and beat until smooth and glossy.

Place well-drained peach or pear halves on an ungreased baking sheet, hollow side up. Place a teaspoon of preserves in each hollow. Cover each half with meringue and sprinkle with nuts. Bake in a slow oven (275°F) one hour or until lightly browned. Remove from pan with a wide spatula. Serve hot or cold. Makes 6.

NUENT

1 cup sugar
½ pound honey
Pinch salt
¼ teaspoon ginger
¼ teaspoon cinnamon
3 cups (12 ounces) chopped walnuts

Do not make on a damp or rainy day or it will be sticky and runny.

Cook honey and sugar over moderate heat about 10 minutes or until golden brown, stirring only until sugar is dissolved. Remove from heat, as overcooking at this point will burn the mixture very quickly. Stir in spices and nuts. Spread on a wet board, platter, or cookie sheet, about ½-inch thick. While still warm, cut into squares or diamonds. Makes about 1½ pounds.

INGBERLACH

2 cups sugar
1 pound honey
1 cup water
Pinch salt
½ teaspoon cinnamon
½ teaspoon ginger
2 cups coarsely chopped walnuts
4 cups matzo farfel

Cook sugar, honey, and water in a large saucepan over low heat for 5 minutes, stirring constantly. Continue cooking over low heat, but do not stir, until a drop of syrup forms a very firm ball when dropped into cold water (255°F on a candy thermometer). Remove from heat. Stir in remaining ingredients. Pour onto greased cookie sheet and spread with spatula. Cool and cut into squares or diamonds. Makes about 3 pounds.

DELICATE PASSOVER TEIGLACH

¼ cup oil or melted shortening
6 tablespoons water
½ teaspoon salt
1 cup matzo meal
2 eggs
1 cup honey
½ cup sugar
1½ teaspoons ginger
½ cup chopped walnuts

In a saucepan, bring oil, water, and salt to a boil. Add matzo meal and blend over low heat until mixture forms a ball and pulls away from the sides of the pan. Remove from heat. Beat in eggs, one at a time, very thoroughly, until dough is smooth. With lightly oiled hands, shape dough into several ½-inch-thick ropes. Cut into ½-inch pieces. Place on well-greased cookie sheets and bake in a hot oven (400°F) 20 minutes or until golden brown. Bring honey, sugar, and ginger to a boil over moderate heat. Add baked teiglach and cook for 15 minutes, stirring occasionally. Stir in nuts and pour onto a wet board or platter to cool.

RECIPE INDEX

INDEX

Appetizers, 38-43
Chicken Livers, Sautéed, 42
Chicken Spread Amandine, 43
Chopped Liver, 42
Crunchy Chicken Spread, 43
Crunchy Spread, 41
Easy Chopped Herring, 40
Fishlet Cocktail, with Horseradish Sauce, 39
Fishlets in Tomato Flower Cups, 39
Garlic-Cheese Spread, 41
Gefilte Fish, 40
Hors d'Oeuvre Puffs, 43
Horseradish Dip, 39
Hot Fish Hors d'Oeuvres, 39
Knishelach, 42
Nippy Fish Canapés, 41
Pickled-Herring and Cream-Cheese Spread, 41
Tangy Tongue Canapés, 43
Walnut-and-Egg Spread, 41
Bananas:
Banana Fritters, 115
Banana-Nut Cookies, 162
Banana-Nut Kugel, 177
Banana-Nut Sponge Cake, 157
Banana Spice Cake, 158
Banana-Nut Chiffon Cake, 150
Fried Bananas, 141
Beef:
Beef Paprika, 55
Beef in Red Wine, 55
Brisket Roast I, 53
Brisket Roast II, 53
Country-Fried Shoulder Steaks, 54
Deborah's Steak Roll-Ups, 53
Easiest-Ever Beef Loaf, 57
Frosted Beef Loaf, 58
Fruited Beef with Fluffy Potato Knaidlach, 54
Holiday Beef Ring, 59
Pot Roast Marinade, 55
Savory Chuck Steak, 54
Stuffed Beefburgers, 63
Swiss Steak, 56
Beets:
Beets à l'Orange, 129
Harvard Beets, 130
Marmalade Beets, 129
Savory Honeyed Beets, 129
Blintzes:
Batter for Blintzes, 107
Cheese Blintzes, 108
Chicken Blintzes with Hot Cranberry Sauce, 111
Chicken-Salad Blintzes, 110
Fruit-Nut-Cheese Blintzes, 109
Liver Blintzes and Tomato-and-Mushroom Sauce, 109
Meat Blintzes, 110
Strawberries-and-Cream Blintzes, 108
Surprise Blintzes, 108
Vegetable-Cheese Blintzes, 109
Borscht, see Soups
Bread substitutes, 171-72
Passover Bagel, 172
Passover Muffins, 171

Passover Rolls, 172
Tzibelle Matzo, 171
Brownies, see Cookies
Brussels Sprouts:
Deborah's Brussels Sprouts, 130
Savory Brussels Sprouts, 130
Cabbage:
Cranberry-Cabbage Relish, 125
Stuffed Cabbage (Holishkes), 62
Cakes, baked from mixes, 156-62
Banana-Nut Sponge Cake, 157
Banana Spice Cake, 158
Chocolate-Dot Sponge Cake, 162
Cinnamon-Raisin Sponge Cake, 161
Coffee Pound Cake, 159
Coffee Sponge Cake, 160
Easy Chiffon Cake, 157
Easy Coffee Chiffon Cake, 158
Easy Nut Cake, 159
Golden Sponge Torte, 161
Jelly Roll, 158
Mocha Sponge Cake, 160
Nut Pound Cake, 159
Rozinkes Mit Mandlen Cake, 158
Spice-Nut Sponge Cake, 161
Sponge Cupcakes, 159
Sponge Layers, 159
Toasted Almond Sponge Cake, 161
Cakes, baked from scratch, 146-52
Apple Crumb Cake, 152
Banana-Nut Chiffon Cake, 150
Cheese Cake, 151
Chiffon Cake, 150
Nine-Egg Passover Sponge Cake, 148
Nut Torte, 149
Potato-Starch Sponge Cake, 149
Refrigerator Loaf Cake, 151
Six-Egg Passover Sponge Cake, 148
Cakes, frostings for:
Coffee Fluff, 160
Coffee Whipped Cream, 160
Canapés, see Appetizers
Carrots:
Carrot Pancakes, 133
Carrot Pudding, 131
Carrot-and-Raisin Salad, 119
Carrot Timbales, 131
Celery and Carrots à l'Athène, 135
Crunchy Harvard Carrots, 133
French-Fried Carrots, 132
Ginger-Honey-Glazed Carrots, 132
Honey-Glazed Carrots, 132
Lyonnaise Carrots, 132
Piquant Carrots, 131
Yom Tov Carrot Ring, 133
Casseroles:
Farfel Chicken Casserole, 83
Fish-and-Egg Casserole, 96
Frankfurter-Sweet Potato-Apple Casserole, 73
Oriental Eggplant Casserole, 102
Potatoes en Casserole, 138
Simple Salmon Casserole, 100
Sweet-Potato-and-Prune Casserole, 140

Cauliflower:
French-Fried Cauliflower, 134
New Orleans Cauliflower, 134

Celery:
Braised Celery, 134
Celery and Carrots à l'Athène, 135
Celery and Mushrooms Amandine, 135
Celery Stuffing, 87

Chicken:
Baked Broilers with Matzo-Nut Stuffing, 79
Baked Chicken with Mushrooms, 77
Broiled Chicken, 80
Chicken à la Princess on Potato Latkes, 84
Chicken Cacciatore, 78
Chicken Cutlets with Tomato-and-Mushroom Sauce, 83
Chicken-Giblet Fricassee, 60
Chicken Livers, Sautéed, 42
Chicken Paprika with Fluffy Potato Knaidlach, 78
Chicken Soup, 44
Epicurean Chicken, 78
Farfel Chicken Casserole, 83
Fried Chicken, 82
Gan Eden Chicken, 79
Glazed Chicken with Matzo-Nut Stuffing, Honeyed Chicken. 80
Hot Chicken Loaf, 84
Lemon Baked Chicken, 80
Oven-Fried Chicken, 82
Pot-Roasted Stuffed Chicken, 77
Smothered Chicken, 79

Cole slaw:
Mariner's Cole Slaw, 122
Special Cole Slaw, 120

Confections, see Sweet things

Cookbook, how to use, 10-11

Cookies, baked from mixes, 156, 162-64
Banana-Nut Cookies, 162
Bull's-Eye Cookies, 164
Chocolate Nut Crisps, 163
Crunchy Nut Cookies, 163
Easy Nut Cookies, 163
Frosted Walnut Crisps, 164
Hermits, 162
Honey Nut Drops, 164
Nut Drop Cookies, 163

Cookies, baked from scratch, 152-55
Almond Drop Cookies, 154
Date-Nut Kisses, 153
Fruit-Nut Chews, 154
Fudge Brownies, 153
Lacy Wafers, 155
Mocha Fudge Brownies, 153
Nut Cookies, 154

Cornish Hens:
Stuffed Rock Cornish Hens, 85

Croquettes:
Delectable Cheese Croquettes, 114
Fishlet Croquettes, 114

Deep-fat frying, 106-7

Desserts, see Cakes; Cookies; Pastries; Sweet things

Dips, see Appetizers

Duck:
Honeyed Duck with Orange Sauce, 86
Orange Braised Duck, 85

Eggplant:
Creole Eggplant, 136
Fried Eggplant, 136
Oriental Eggplant Casserole, 102
Spanish Eggplant, 135

Eggs:
Cream-Cheese Scrambled Eggs, 92
Creamy Marmalade Omelet, 91
Denver Sandwiches, 93
Light-as-a-Feather Omelet, 92
Matzo-Meal Omelet, 92
Neptune Egg Scramble, 93
Savory Eggs and Frankfurters, 93
Spanish Egg Surprise, 91

Farfel:
Farfel Ring, 144
Savory Matzo Farfel, 144
Toasted Matzo Farfel, 49

Fish:
Baked Fish and Vegetables, 95
Busy-Day Fish Bake, 96
Cheese-Fried Fish, 94
Crunchy Potato-Fried Fish, 94
Fish-and-Egg Casserole, 96
Fish Fillets Amandine, 95
Fisherman's Potato Pancakes, 98
Fried Fillets of Flounder, 94
Gefilte-Fish Sauté, 97
Gourmet Salmon Loaf, 99
Salmon Cutlets, 100
Salmon Loaf, 99
Savory Fish in Potato Nests, 98
Simple Salmon Casserole, 100
Yom Tov Fish Mousse, 97

Fish, sauces for:
Buttery Lemon Sauce, 100
Cucumber Sauce for Gefilte Fish, 124
Dill Sauce, 97
Wine-Butter Sauce, 101

Frankfurters:
Frankfurter-Sweet Potato-Apple Casserole, 73
Savory Eggs and Frankfurters, 93

Fried things, 106-15
see also specific names of dishes

Fritters:
Apple Fritters, 114
Banana Fritters, 115

Frostings, cake, see Cakes, frostings for

Gefilte fish, 40
Busy-Day Fish Bake, 96
Fish-and-Egg Casserole, 96
Fisherman's Potato Pancakes, 98
Gefilte-Fish Sauté, 97
Savory Fish in Potato Nests, 98
Yom Tov Fish Mousse, 97

Halke, 56

Herring:
Easy Chopped Herring, 40
Pickled-Herring and Cream-Cheese Spread, 41

Hors d'Oeuvres, see Appetizers

Ingredients made by Manischewitz, 12-13
Knaidlach, Fluffy Potato, 50
Chicken Paprika with, 78
Fruited Beef with, 54
Knishelach, 42
"Kosher for Passover" labeled foods and cleaning supplies, 14
Kugel:
Apple Matzo Kugel, 178
Banana-Nut Kugel, 177
Easiest Potato Kugel, 142
Easy "Grated" Potato Kugel, 143
Matzo-Cheese Kugel, 101
Matzo Kugel, 143
Matzo Meal Kugel, 143
Potato-Cheese Kugel, 101
Potato Kugelach, 142
Lamb:
Braised Lamb Shanks, 69
Festive Braised Lamb Chops, 69
Lamb Chops à l'Orange, 69
Lamb Chops Creole, 66
Lamb Chops and Potato Bake, 70
Lamb Chops on Prune Stuffing, 68
Shish Kebabs, 68
Spiced Lamb Shanks, 67
Stuffed Breast of Lamb, 67
Sweet-and-Sour Lamb Tongues, 71
Latkes:
Cheese Latkes, 113
Coconut Latkes, 112
Luncheon Latkes, 113
Matzo-Meal Latkes, 111
Potato Latkes, 112
   Chicken à la Princess on, 84
Salami Latkes, 113
White-and-Gold Potato Latkes, 112
Liver:
Braised Liver, 72
Chicken Livers, Sautéed, 42
Chopped Liver, 42
Festive Liver Ring, 72
Liver Blintzes with Tomato-and-Mushroom Sauce, 109
Liver Cutlets, 71
Matzo balls, 47-49
Crunchy Stuffing Balls, 144
Economy Matzo Balls, 49
Firm Matzo Balls, 48
Fluffy Matzo Balls, 48
Traditional Matzo Balls, 48
Matzo Brei, 103
Measuring ingredients, 11
Meat Cups, 62
Meat Loaf:
Applesauce Meat Loaf, 57
Easiest-Ever Beef Loaf, 57
Frosted Beef Loaf, 58
Hidden-Treasure Meat Loaf, 57
Jiffy Meat Loaf, 58
Pinwheel Meat Loaf, 58
Surprise Meat Loaf, 59

Sweet-and-Sour Meat Loaf, 59
Meatballs:
Surprise Klops, 60
Sweet-and-Sour Meatballs, 61
Yom Tov Meatballs, 61
Meats, 52-73
see also specific names of meats
Miltz, Stuffed, 73
Onions:
Golden Onion Soup, 44
Onion Sauce, 71
Oven temperatures, 11-12
Passover:
house, preparation of, 20-21
how to set Seder table, 22-23
menu planning, 24
    Seder suggestions, 26-28
    breakfasts, 29-30
    luncheons or suppers, 31-32
    dinners, 33-35
Pastries, 165-70
Coffee-Banana Cream Pie, 169
Crunchy Cream-Cheese Tarts, 167
Date-Cheese Pie, 168
Lemon Meringue Pie, 168
Matzo-Meal Pie Crust, 167
Mocha Cream Pie, 167
Peach of a Lemon Pie, 169
Petite Jam Tarts, 166
Puff Shells, 170
Strawberries-and-Cream Pie, 169
Strawberry-Cream Tarts, 166
Peppers:
Stuffed Peppers, 63
Veal with Peppers, 64
Pies, see Pastries
Potatoes:
Crusty Roasted Potatoes, 139
Easiest Potato Kugel, 142
Easy "Grated" Potato Kugel, 143
Fisherman's Potato Pancakes, 98
Golden Parsley Potatoes, 138
Potato-Cheese Kugel, 101
Potato Kugelach, 142
Potato Latkes, 112
Potato Soup Verde, 45
Potatoes en Casserole, 138
Prune-and-Potato Tzimmes, 138
Scalloped Potatoes in Tomato Sauce, 137
White-and-Gold Potato Latkes, 112
see also Sweet potatoes
Pots and pans, selecting of, 11
Poultry, 76-87
see also Chicken; Cornish Hens; Duck
Poultry stuffing, 86-87
Basic Matzo Stuffing, 86
   Variations, 87
Cranberry Stuffing, 87
Matzo-Nut Stuffing, 79, 81
Parsley Stuffing, 87
Puffs:
Cheese-Mushroom Puff, 102

RECIPE INDEX

Hors d'Oeuvre Puffs, 43
Puff Shells, 170

Relishes:
Almond-Cranberry Sauce, 125
Cranberry-Apple Relish, 125
Cranberry-Cabbage Relish, 125

Salad Dressings:
French Dressing, 124
Horseradish Dressing, 121
Ruby Salad Dressing, 123
Russian Dressing, 123
Sour-Cream Dressing, 124

Salads:
Carrot-and-Raisin Salad, 119
Crisp-and-Tart Chicken Salad, 123
Cucumber Salad, 119
Fishlet Boats, 121
Hearty Supper Salad, 121
Mariner's Cole Slaw, 122
Shicker's Chicken Salad, 122
Snappy Fish Salad, 122
Special Cole Slaw, 120
Supper Waldorf Salad, 120
Tossed Lettuce and Tomatoes, 119
Waldorf Salad, 120

Salmon:
Gourmet Salmon Loaf, 99
Salmon Cutlets, 100
Salmon Loaf, 99
Simple Salmon Casserole, 100

Sauces:
Almond-Cranberry Sauce, 125
Almond-Raisin Sauce for Tongue, 70
Apricot-Raisin Sauce for Tongue, 70
Cucumber Sauce for Gefilte Fish, 124
Dessert Wine Sauce, 175
Horseradish Sauce, 39
Onion Sauce, 71
Orange Sauce for Duck, 86
Sauce Piquant for Veal, 65
Spicy Fruit Sauce, 179
Velvet Vegetable Sauce, 142
see also Fish, sauces for

Sauté, definition of, 106

Shish Kebabs, 68

Soup accessories, 47-50
Fluffy Potato Knaidlach, 50
Matzo Balls, 48-49
Passover Mandlen, 49
Passover Noodles, 50
Toasted Matzo Farfel, 49

Soups, 44-46
Borscht Bisque, 46
Borscht Buttermilk Shake, 46
Borscht Frost, 46
Borscht Levantine, 46
Borscht Shake, 46
Chicken Soup, 44
Fresh Tomato Soup, 45
Golden Onion Soup, 44
Hamishe Vegetable Soup, 45
Potato Soup Verde, 45
Spring Vegetable Soup, 44

Spinach:
Creamed Spinach, 137
Sweet-and-Sour Spinach, 136

Spreads:
Chicken Spread Amandine, 43
Crunchy Chicken Spread, 43
Crunchy Spread, 41
Garlic-Cheese Spread, 41
Pickled-Herring and Cream-Cheese Spread, 41
Walnut-and-Egg Spread, 41

Stuffing, see Poultry stuffing

Sweet potatoes:
Cranberry-Glazed Sweet Potatoes, 139
Frankfurter-Sweet Potato-Apple Casserole, 73
Honeyed Sweet Potatoes, 140
Orange-Glazed Sweet Potatoes, 140
Sweet-Potato-and-Applesauce Pudding, 139

Sweet-Potato-and-Prune Casserole, 140

Sweet things, 174-80
Apple-Crumb Pudding, 178
Apple Matzo Kugel, 178
Banana-Nut Kugel, 177
Creamy Mocha Shalet, 177
Crunchy Apple-Orange Meichel, 179
Delicate Passover Teiglach, 180
Dessert Wine Sauce, 175
Fruit Meringue Charlotte, 177
Fruit Meringues, 179
Gourmet Parfait, 175
Ingberlach, 180
Lemon Meringue Charlotte, 176
Mocha Pudding, 176
Nuent, 180
Peach Shalet, 176
Pears Concord, 179
Spicy Fruit Sauce, 179
Sweet-Potato-and-Applesauce Pudding, 139
see also Cakes; Cookies; Pastries

Tarts, see Pastries

Tomatoes:
Fresh Tomato Soup, 45
Scalloped Tomatoes, 137
Tossed Lettuce and Tomatoes, 119

Tzimmes:
Prune-and-Potato Tzimmes, 138
Tzimmes with Halke, 56

Veal:
Breaded Veal Cutlet, 66
Creole Veal Cutlets, 66
Stuffed Breast of Veal, 65
Tomato Veal Cutlets, 64
Veal Nuggets with Sauce Piquant, 65
Veal with Peppers, 64
Veal Roll, 64
Veal Rolls Sauterne, 66
Veal Sauterne, 63

Vegetables, 128-44
Hamishe Vegetable Soup, 45
Spring Garden Vegetables, 141
Spring Vegetable Soup, 44
Vegetable Medley, 141
Velvet Vegetable Sauce, 142
see also specific names of vegetables